INSIGHT POCKET GUIDE

Santa Fe
TAOS · ALBUQUERQUE

Discovery CHANNEL

APA PUBLICATIONS
Part of the Langenscheidt Publishing Group

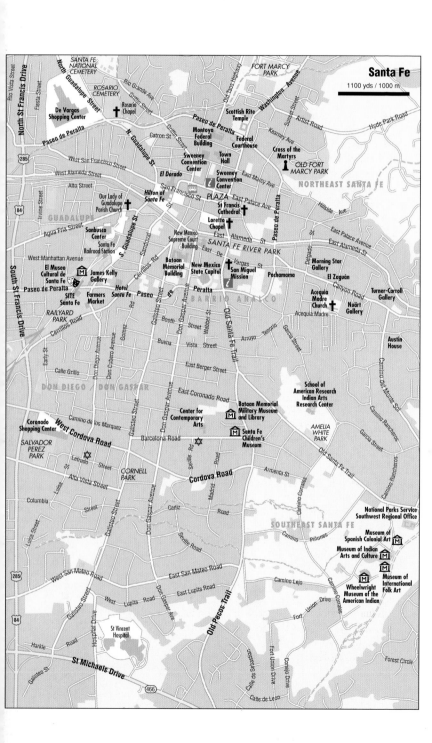

introduction

Welcome

This guidebook combines the interests and enthusiasms of two of the world's best-known information providers: Insight Guides, which has set the standard for visual travel guides since 1970, and Discovery Channel, the world's premier source of nonfiction television programming. Its aim is to provide the best of Santa Fe and its surroundings in the course of seven city itineraries and five out-of-town excursions.

From its origins as a frontier Hispanic town founded atop ancient Indian pueblos, to its emergence as one of modern America's most authentic multicultural cities, Santa Fe regularly tops the list of favorite destinations in the US. The itineraries in this guide, devised by Nicky Leach, Insight's expert on the Southwest, explore the museums, historic buildings, theaters, and attractions in downtown Santa Fe, then move on to the mountains and country attractions that surround the 'City Different,' like the celebrity hideout of Tesuque, a pretty Hispanic village, 9 miles (14km) from Downtown, and the world-famous Santa Fe Opera. Longer excursions take in the overland loop road to artsy Taos, the ski resorts on the Colorado border, and the historic Santa Fe Trail. The landscape made famous by Georgia O'Keeffe and a scenic detour through mining ghost towns to the state's largest city, Albuquerque, form the final excursions in the book.

The itineraries are supported by sections on history and culture, eating out, shopping, and nightlight, plus a calendar of special events. At the end, a practical information section covers transportation, communications, money, etc., including a list of recommended hotels at all price levels.

Nicky Leach, an award-winning writer and editor who specializes in nature and heritage travel in the US, has lived in Santa Fe since 1990. A contributor and editor for more than a dozen Insight Guide/Discovery Channel guides, she was the principal author on the in-depth companion volume to this book: *Insight Guide: New Mexico*.

Leach was particularly pleased to be asked to play tour guide to Santa Fe, which she considers offers an unparalleled quality of life for such a small city. 'It was fun to share my insider's perspective on Santa Fe,' she says. 'It takes time to get to know this subtle place, where you're not a local until your family has lived here for generations.'

HISTORY AND CULTURE

Santa Fe is the oldest state capital in the United States, with the threads of several cultures – Indian, Spanish, Mexican, and American – instrumental in making it one of America's most artistic and distinctive towns.......**11–17**

CITY AND AREA ITINERARIES

The first five tours link Santa Fe's essential sights, and give recommendations on where to eat along the way. The next two itineraries take in attractions in the areas surrounding the city.

1   Downtown Santa Fe concentrates on the four blocks surrounding the historic Plaza, including the Palace of the Governors and St Francis Cathedral. The area has several museums to explore, like the Museum of Fine Arts, the Georgia O'Keeffe Museum, and the Indian-run Institute of American Indian Arts...**22**

2   Museum Hill lies near the Old Santa Fe Trail. Its attractions include the Museum of International Folk Art, the Santa Fe Children's Museum, the Museum of Indian Arts and Culture, and the Wheelwright Museum of the American Indian **27**

3   Canyon Road focuses on Santa Fe's arts district. After visiting galleries, the tour goes to El Zaguán, the oldest artist's residence, then to other houses built or lived in by creative residents. One of them is the Randall Davey Audubon Center, a wonderful place to walk or hike ...**31**

4   Barrio Analco is a half-day walking tour of the city's oldest neighborhood, visiting the State Capitol building and ending up in the Pink Adobe Restaurant **35**

5   Guadalupe-Railyards Historic District is Santa Fe's trendy warehouse area. Begin at the Farmer's Market, then spend time shopping, sightseeing, and taking in a movie after dinner...**37**

6   Tesuque, the Ski Basin and the Santa Fe Opera leaves Santa Fe for the Sangre de Cristo Mountains, where you can ski, hike, visit the Hispanic village of Tesuque, or soak in a hot tub at the Ten Thousand Waves spa. End the trip with a visit to the Santa Fe Opera **39**

7   Santa Fe Area Pueblos and the Jémez Mountains visits ancient and contemporary Indian pueblos, goes to Los Alamos, the birthplace of the atom bomb, and to Bandelier National Monument. Study a collaped volcano caldera, and enjoy a steamy massage...........................**41**

contents

EXCURSIONS

Five road tours focus on Taos, Albuquerque, and the attractions of northeastern New Mexico, all within a day's drive of Santa Fe.

1 The **High Road to Taos** leads to the neighborhoods of Chimayó, white-water rafts down the Rio Grande Gorge, and visits the 'Lourdes of America' **51**

2 **Taos and the Enchanted Circle** travels to the Kit Carson Home, and includes a stroll through the streets of free-spirited Taos. After Taos Pueblo, take the Enchanted Circle route to the D.H. Lawrence Ranch **55**

3 **O'Keeffe Country** takes an up-close-and-personal look at the landscapes and Hispanic farming villages that inspired the USA's most famous 20th-century artist ...**62**

4 The **Santa Fe Trail** traces the historic route and takes in the Victorian town of Las Vegas, a former US Army fort, Old West towns, a volcano, and wildlife **67**

5 The **Turquoise Trail to Albuquerque** travels to New Mexico's largest city via old mining ghost towns. Once in Albuquerque, go to museums, the historic Plaza, the KiMo Theater, and take a trip down Route 66 ....**72**

LEISURE ACTIVITIES

Where to eat, shop, and unwind in New Mexico...**77–86**

CALENDAR OF EVENTS

A guide to festivals in New Mexico **87**

PRACTICAL INFORMATION

All the background information you are likely to need for your stay in New Mexico. Includes ideas on where to stay, from famous hotels to bed & breakfast inns **89–99**

MAPS

Santa Fe **4**	*Northeastern*
Central Santa Fe ...**18–19**	*New Mexico* **48–49**
Museum Hill and	*Taos* **56**
Canyon Road **30**	*Albuquerque* **74**
Around Santa Fe **40**	

INDEX AND CREDITS

pages **101–104**

Preceding Pages: artist Georgia O'Keeffe's 'hidden' ranch, Abiquíu
Following Pages: turquoise and silver, Albuquerque

History & Culture

I n 2002–03, a high-profile excavation behind Santa Fe's Palace of the Governors uncovered more than 195,000 artifacts, from bones to pots, in four separate layers many feet below ground level. The sheer number of artifacts discovered was not unexpected. It had long been known the Palace originally extended two blocks north. Over the centuries, the site had been an Indian pueblo, Spanish and American army barracks, offices, a prison, and a post office, among other things. In fact, every time workers dig in downtown Santa Fe, they unearth relics dating back to the 18th and 19th centuries.

The biggest surprise, though, was the date of the oldest European artifacts found: 1603. Until then, it had been thought that Santa Fe, the oldest state capital in the US, had been founded *circa* 1610. The new date is the clearest evidence yet that Santa Fe is even older than once thought. Stories like these illustrate the city's extraordinary antiquity. Most towns in the American West were founded in the mid-1800s as overnight boom towns associated with big mining strikes. But Santa Fe was already two centuries old and set in its ways when Americans started coming West to seek their fortunes. Its greatest changes began when it passed from Spanish to Mexican rule in 1821, and thousands of explorers, traders, and immigrants traveled the 900-mile (1,450-km) Santa Fe Trail from Franklin, Missouri, to Santa Fe and beyond. Even then, travel by wagon on much of the trail was only for the dedicated.

Nearby mining towns like Cerrillos on the Turquoise Trail, founded atop prehistoric Indian mines by the first Spanish settlers, grew overnight with the 1880 arrival of the railroad. Santa Fe was, ironically, saved from a similar fate, when the main transcontinental railroad bypassed the town in favor of Albuquerque, which then started its rise to boom city of the future.

It could be argued that it was at that point that Santa Fe's persona as a city that looked back not forward was sealed. As historians, archeologists, artists and architects, and well-educated patrons found their way to Taos and Santa Fe in the early 1900s, the City Different, as it is now known, came to stand for something disappearing quickly from the rest of America: a multicultural society that celebrates and preserves centuries-old traditions.

Prehistoric Cultures

The threads of three cultures – Indian, Hispanic, and 'Anglo' *(see page 91)* – run through Santa Fe and New Mexico. Of these by far the oldest is American Indian, which dates back at least 12,000 years to the time when Clovis hunters pursued game in eastern New Mexico at the end of the Ice Age. About 2,500 years ago, when corn and later squash and beans were introduced from Mexico, late Archaic hunter-gatherers

Left: a Zuni man, around 1903
Right: exhibit from the Art of Ancient America, Governor's Palace

became farmers. Labor-intensive farming required a more sedentary lifestyle, sowing seed, irrigating, watching over fields, and harvesting at the right time.

By AD700, families had graduated from living in underground pithouses to small pueblos of above-ground masonry houses made of mortared stones covered in mud adobe. Their old subterranean homes were now incorporated

as underground ceremonial rooms, or *kivas.* As long droughts began to affect crops, ritual specialists met in the kivas and plotted the movements of the sun, moon, and planets every day, then announced times for planting and harvesting ceremonies.

In the 11th century, priests in the San Juan Basin in northwestern New Mexico became powerful leaders presiding over a vast trade network throughout the Southwest, Mexico, the Mississippi River valley, and the Pacific. But drought was the enemy.

By 1300, Pueblo were moving to be near to the Rio Grande and its tributaries. At the time of their first contact with Spanish conquistador Don Francisco Vasquez de Coronado, in 1540, the 70 or so pueblos that had survived ongoing water shortages were self-sufficient city-states made up of clans who had migrated from elsewhere. Each pueblo had specialized pottery, clothing, food, and tools, which could be used in trade, much as they are today.

Hispanic Heritage

New Mexico was unlike anywhere else under Spanish colonial rule. It lay on a wild frontier, so far north of Mexico City, the capital of New Spain, everyone was forced to improvise. Administrators interpreted government orders according to the needs of the new land yet maintained the appearance of conformity. This pragmatic operational style remains a hallmark of Santa Fe today, where an emphasis on often seemingly capricious rules drags out official business, and citizens are forced to find creative ways to get things done.

When New Mexico's first governor, the cruel and ambitious Don Juan de Oñate, was relieved of his post around 1600, Don Pedro de Peralta, his successor, was left to begin anew. Accompanied by soldiers, missionaries, and settlers, he laid out Santa Fe atop the ruined pueblo of Ogapoge. La Villa Real de Santa Fe probably followed the traditional royal *ordenanza plan*: a large, defensible plaza, twice as long as it was wide, surrounded by churches, administrative buildings, and homes, with communal fields irrigated by ditches, or *acequias,* on the outskirts – a layout still found in some New Mexican villages.

As planned, the colonial plaza in Santa Fe stretched as far as today's St Francis Cathedral, a block east of the Plaza, and had eight streets running from it: two on each corner and one from the center of each long side. A handful of Spanish families built their homes around the Plaza, north of the Santa Fe

Above: archeological remains at Bandelier National Monument

River, and reserved the area south of the river (the Barrio Analco) for their Mexican Indian and African slaves. Churches served each community, and administrators in the Casas Reales (Royal Houses), later called the Palace of the Governors, ruled New Mexico from the north side of the Plaza.

Missionary Fervor

Missionaries targeted pueblos for large missions aimed at converting Indian residents to Catholicism. A priest would petition the pueblo leader, or *cacique*, for entry and usually receive a building for use as a residence and church. Neophytes then assisted the priest in building a large, elaborate church with adjoining *convento*, or residence, and pastures and fields. The fathers then introduced fruit and wheat farming, breadmaking in a Moorish-style outdoor beehive oven known as an *horno* in Spanish, silversmithing, and cattle for meat, candle tallow, tanned hide, glue, and other products introduced from Europe.

Spanish settlers and missionary priests each required the pueblos to pay tribute, or *encomienda*, annually, in the form of a certain number of bushels of corn and woven cotton cloth, or *mantas*. In theory, Indian labor was to be compensated. In practice, this rarely happened, and Pueblos exhausted themselves working for their rulers and growing enough corn and cotton for themselves, Indian trading partners, and the Spaniards.

New Mexico natives found themselves caught between church and state. Both relied on Indians to supplement scarce supplies from Mexico City, which arrived once every three years. By 1680, the Pueblos had had enough. Led by Popé, an elder from San Juan, they rose up against their oppressors, killing the Spanish priests and expelling Spanish settlers south to El Paso, Texas.

When Don Diego de Vargas and his followers reconquered New Mexico in 1693, relations between the Spaniards and Pueblos changed. After an initial struggle, the Pueblos gave in to Spanish rule. In return, the Spaniards abolished *encomienda* and adopted a policy of tolerance toward Indian religion.

Spanish law now still acknowledges the sovereignty of each pueblo, and the rights of residents to carry out their religious observances. And in time, Pueblos and

Top: Don Diego de Vargas
Right: rock art showing Spanish soldiers

Spaniards became united against a new mutual enemy: bands of marauding Apaches, Navajos, Utes, and Comanches moving south into New Mexico after being pushed off their lands by American settlers moving west.

Mexico won independence from Spain in 1821. Within months, New Mexicans – now ruled by a Mexican governor – were welcoming American traders arriving in Santa Fe from Missouri along the Santa Fe Trail. Even as a flood of trade goods arrived by the wagon load, the villages were left to their own devices by the Catholic church.

By 1846, relations between the United States and Mexico had deteriorated into war. In June, American trader Samuel Magoffin and his wife Susan traveled the Santa Fe Trail to do business in Santa Fe and arrived just as the state capital was being peacefully occupied by the US Army of the West under Gen. Stephen Kearny. Two years later, Mexico formally ceded the Southwest to the US under the Treaty of Guadalupe-Hidalgo and New Mexico became American territory.

American Manifest Destiny

Under American territorial rule (1850–1912), Santa Fe underwent a huge shift in its population from a large Hispanic majority to increasing numbers of Anglos (a word in New Mexico that historically refers to all non-Hispanic people). The US Army had a strong presence at Fort Marcy, just north of the Plaza. More soldiers were based at Fort Union, in northeastern New Mexico, where they protected travelers on the Santa Fe Trail from Indian depredations.

French-born Bishop Jean-Baptiste Lamy became head of the Catholic church in New Mexico and moved swiftly to impose the mainstream church on the folk religion that had taken hold during the Mexican period. In Santa Fe, Lamy built European-style churches and the first schools and colleges.

In villages such as Abiquiu, priests were forced to toe the line or be excommunicated – an action that drove the folk religion underground, where it remains today, shrouded in secrecy.

The first American governor, Charles Bent, a former mountain man and colleague of Kit Carson, was murdered in his Taos home a year after taking office by Indians and Hispanics opposed to American rule. By the time the last two territorial governors, Lew Wallace and Bradford Prince, occupied the now decrepit, much-

Top: Atchison, Topeka & Santa Fe, 1881
Right: awaiting statehood, 1911

remodeled Palace of the Governors, at the end of the 1800s, the old adobe building was viewed as an embarassing anachronism, synonymous with an Indian and Hispanic past that held back statehood.

A fortuitous set of circumstances saved Santa Fe from obscurity at the beginning of the 20th century. The Victorian love of antiquities and the arrival of the railroad in New Mexico in 1880 had captured the attention of amateur archeologists and anthropologists like Adolph Bandelier and educator Edgar Lee Hewett, and railroad tourism and hotel entrepreneur Fred Harvey, among others. As World War I loomed, wealthy and well-educated Americans no longer vacationed in Europe and were rediscovering their own country, helped by modern transportation, tourist guides, and a fascination with Indian cultures that were thought to be dying out.

Santa Fe Style

Hewett followed up Bandelier's studies at New Mexico pueblos by instigating his own under the auspices of the western branch of the School of American Archeology, headquartered in the Palace of the Governors. Together, Hewett, Bradford Prince, and a young archeologist named Jesse Nusbaum restored the palace to its Spanish-Pueblo architecture in 1909. They then collaborated with Colorado architect Isaac Rapp to invent a completely new style for Santa Fe that drew on its Pueblo and Spanish heritage.

In 1912, New Mexico achieved statehood, and Santa Fe retained not only the state capitol but captured the interest of artists drawn to the desert to heal tuberculosis contracted in industrial cities back east. Both Taos and Santa Fe became known as arts colonies, with each town competing to host international celebrity thinkers like writer D.H. Lawrence and Carl Jung. During World War II, government work at Los Alamos building the first nuclear bomb put lightly populated New Mexico on the map as one of the top places for technological research in the world. After the war many scientists stayed and, with a growing number of writers and artists, played an active role in Santa Fe life, including preserving the city through tough new architectural laws.

In the late 1930s, auto traffic received a boost with the routing of the cross-country Route 66 through Albuquerque and Santa Fe. Visitation increased in the decades following World War II, as Route 66 gave way to fast, new interstates linking the country. A new group of hippies, New Agers, and counter-culturalists moved to Santa Fe and Taos in the 1960s and 1970s, attracted by the same things that had brought earlier Bohemians and still attract people today: a beautiful landscape, interesting cultures, tolerance of differences, friendly small-town life, and affordable property.

Right: J.R. Oppenheimer and Gen. Leslie Groves at Los Alamos A bomb test site

That all changed in the 1980s, when growing tourism and wealthy new Anglo residents were attracted to Santa Fe by magazine articles touting the city as 'the next best place.' Determined not to be run out of towns and villages founded by their ancestors, Hispanics and Indians made inroads into politics, social services, and the increasingly lucrative art world, taking back control of their communities, supported by Anglo activists, community grants, and growing political support at the federal government level.

Santa Fe Today

Few places in the West have escaped the pervasive homogenized American culture as successfully as Santa Fe. It remains, primarily, an Hispanic town, where numerous families speak Spanish as their first language and look with pride on four centuries of residency. Many celebrations throughout the year, native foods, dress, and customs have their roots in Spanish Colonial times. Although first-time visitors sometimes dismiss Santa Fe as an 'adobe Disneyland,' with museum Indians, colorful Hispanics, and somber Indian vendors, residents know that the city defies such categorizations. The real Santa Fe lies beyond superficial appearances and takes time and observation to appreciate.

You can experience it in the blood-red hue of the Sangre de Cristo Mountains at sunset, which casts a warm, chile-red glow over low adobe buildings in the city that takes the breath away. You'll encounter it on any Saturday morning at the Santa Fe Farmer's Market in the converted Railyards, where you'll meet not only Hispanic, Pueblo, and Anglo farmers but listen to marimba music by youngsters whose parents hail from Tibet, Indonesia, and the Caribbean.

You'll see it in the passionate concerns of residents, coming together through the arts, politics, charity events, architectural review boards, and water conservation meetings to improve the quality of life in this arid desert town. But most of all, you'll experience a strange kind of well-being that occurs when you least expect it. This is the *duende* – the timeless magic – of Santa Fe, a quality no amount of money can buy and that remains its most precious asset.

history/culture

HISTORY HIGHLIGHTS

AD1150–1400 Pueblos along the Rio Grande and its tributaries are established, following the Great Drought of 1276–99.

Early 1400s Drought causes Indians to abandon the villages closest to Santa Fe and move to other Rio Grande pueblos.

1540 Francisco Vasquez de Coronado goes on an expedition north of Mexico which encounters Pueblo civilization.

1598 The first Spanish colony in New Mexico is founded near San Juan Pueblo, northwest of Santa Fe, by Juan de Oñate.

Early 1600s Santa Fe, the oldest state capital in the US, is established by Onate's successor, Pedro de Peralta, as Spain's northernmost administrative capital in the Southwest. The Casas Reales, or Palace of the Governors is built.

1680 Indian uprising known as the Pueblo Revolt forces the Spanish over the border to El Paso, Texas.

1693 Don Diego de Vargas brings a Spanish military expedition back to Santa Fe and reclaims Santa Fe for the Spanish crown without bloodshed.

1693–96 De Vargas returns to Santa Fe with settlers, but is forced to fight Indians for the Reconquest of New Mexico.

1706 Albuquerque is founded.

1712 Santa Fe celebrates its first Fiesta in thanksgiving for the Reconquest.

1778 Juan Bautista de Anza becomes governor of New Mexico and makes peace with the Comanches.

1807 American explorer Zebulon Pike is arrested in Colorado and incarcerated in Santa Fe. His published account encourages American expansionism.

1821 Mexico wins independence from Spain. William Becknell arrives in Santa Fe, opening up the Santa Fe Trail between Missouri and New Mexico.

1846 The US declares war on Mexico. US Army Gen. Stephen Kearny peacefully occupies Santa Fe after Mexican governor Manuel Armijo flees.

1847 New Mexico's first US governor, Charles Bent, is assassinated in Taos in an Indian and Mexican uprising.

1848 Mexican War ends; Treaty of Guadalupe Hidalgo authorizes US takeover of Southwest.

1850 Congress creates the Territory of New Mexico.

1851 Bishop Jean Baptiste Lamy arrives in Santa Fe and founds the first English-language school.

1862 Confederate troops invade Santa Fe and occupy the Palace of the Governors. The Battle of Glorieta, southeast of Santa Fe, ends Confederate control of New Mexico.

1869 Construction of St Francis Cathedral begins in Santa Fe.

1879 Gov. Lew Wallace writes his novel *Ben Hur* in the Palace of the Governors.

1880 The Atchison, Topeka & Santa Fe Railroad arrives in Santa Fe.

1907 The Palace of the Governors, saved from demolition, becomes headquarters for the Museum of New Mexico and School of American Archeology.

1909 Restoration of the Palace by Edgar Lee Hewitt creates Santa Fe Style.

1912 New Mexico achieves statehood.

1917 Isaac H. Rapp designs the Museum of Fine Arts, the first public Santa Fe Style building.

1926 Artist Will Shuster starts a 'protest fiesta' that includes the burning of the puppet Zozobra, or Old Man Gloom.

1942 Los Alamos is chosen as a nuclear research facility as part of the top-secret Manhattan Project.

1945 Scientists working in Los Alamos produce the world's first atomic bomb.

1957 Santa Fe adopts its Historic District ordinance to help protect landmark buildings. Santa Fe Opera is founded.

1966 New Mexico's present state capital is dedicated in Santa Fe.

1980s Celebrities 'discover' Santa Fe. Prices climb. New Age seekers establish the city as a spiritual center.

2000 The combined population of Santa Fe reaches 163,000.

2002–03 An excavation behind the Palace of the Governors unearths 195,000 artifacts of importance.

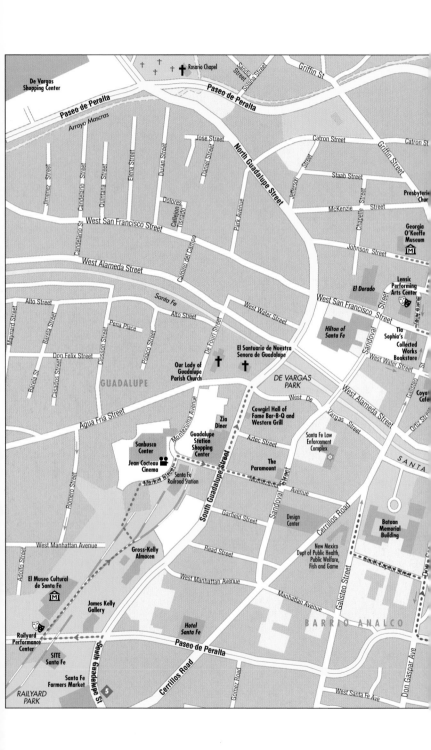

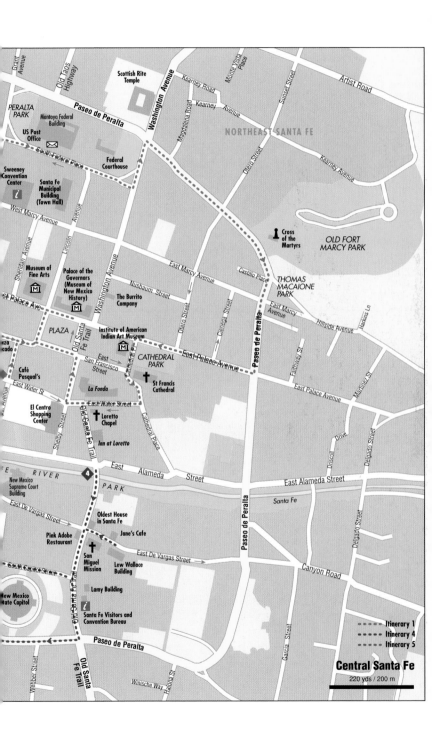

Central Santa Fe

220 yds / 200 m

Itinerary 1
Itinerary 4
Itinerary 5

Orientation

Santa Fe is located in northern New Mexico, nestled in the towering foothills of the Sangre de Cristo Mountains, which soar a mile above the town. With a combined city and county population of 131,000, the 'City Different,' as it is known, has grown considerably since it was founded in the early 1600s as the tiny, remote northern capital of New Spain. But strong preservation laws in the early 20th century created one of the country's most extensive historic districts, all of which can be visited on foot, using the first five itineraries in this guide.

The next two tours take in the country sights around the city, while the last five itineraries travel farther afield, and offer a variety of recreational possibilities – white-water rafting or taking a narrow-gauge railroad ride, enjoying migratory birds and hot-springs, or seeing the attractions in artsy Taos and busy Albuquerque, including Route 66. These excursions require a vehicle, or joining one of the van tours offered by companies in Santa Fe.

My most important advice for visitors to downtown Santa Fe is to park your car immediately and begin to walk. Downtown Santa Fe's narrow winding streets follow former wagon roads associated with the Santa Fe Trail, the overland commercial trail that linked New Mexico with American markets back east between 1821 and 1880. They were never meant for modern cars. Or leave your car at your hotel and ride to town on public transportation or by cab. The least expensive option, the Santa Fe Trails bus system (tel: 505/955-2001), can take you almost anywhere Downtown on any of seven different routes. Buses run roughly every 45 minutes, beginning at the Downtown transit center on Sheridan, and taking in the surrounding areas.

Lastly, allow yourself plenty of time to enjoy Santa Fe – one of America's most extraordinary small cities. If it's your first time, I'd suggest staying in a downtown hotel. You'll be able to immerse yourself in Santa Fe's unique tri-cultural atmosphere and walk most places. There are many choices, but I like the elegant Hotel Santa Fe, one of the city's best deals, five blocks from the Plaza. It's majority owned by Picurís Pueblo and has unique Indian offerings, from nightly flute music and weekly

history lectures to a gourmet restaurant serving food inspired by Native America. The Inn at Loretto is even closer to the Plaza. In summer, you can take the inexpensive Loretto Line Tram (daily Apr–Oct 10am, noon, 2pm; tel: 505/983-3701; no reservations required), which offers a city overview tour that allows you to decide which sights are of most interest.

Left: sculpture outside Santa Fe's Museum of Indian Arts and Culture
Right: Horse Feathers Cowboy Boutique, Taos

City Itineraries

1. DOWNTOWN SANTA FE *(see map, p18)*

This tour concentrates on the attractions in the four blocks surrounding the historic Plaza. There's lots to see and do in this compact area, so pace yourself and take breaks throughout the day in the many pleasant cafés and stores located in historic buildings along the winding streets.

In Mexico, they say *Panza lleno, corazon contento* ('full stomach, contented heart'.) That's the motto of **Café Pasqual** (tel: 505/983-9340), on the corner of Water and Don Gaspar, a perfect place to eat breakfast on your first day in Santa Fe. The décor and cuisine at Katherine Kagel's tiny but sophisticated eatery draws heavily on Mexico. Don't miss the *huevos rancheros* – they're some of the best around. Mexican tilework, images of San Pasqual (patron saint of the kitchen), and colorful paper banners complete the air of perpetual fiesta.

After breakfast, walk to the **Plaza**, one block east and one block north of Café Pasqual. The Plaza has changed a lot over the last 400 years. For one thing, it's now smaller than other Spanish colonial plazas, which were laid out in accordance with strict royal guidelines. Nor is the modern Plaza the daily meeting place it once was, when locals did all their shopping at downtown mercantiles.

But even as the city has expanded outwards over the years, and ordinary folks have been priced out of their city center, the Plaza itself has remained the heart and soul of Santa Fe. Locals still give downtown directions stating how many blocks from the Plaza a given location is, and it's still the important place for community get-togethers – from Christmas festivities to

city itineraries

summer's Spanish and Indian markets, the oldest and largest such street festivals in the country.

In the downtown core, buildings are required to conform to either Spanish Pueblo Mission or Territorial adobe style.

The building that inspired the drive to return Santa Fe to its original Spanish-style architecture is on the Plaza's north side. The Spanish Pueblo-style **Palace of the Governors**, or Casas Reales (Royal Houses), was built in the early 1600s, and is the oldest government administration building in the US. It has been home to 60 Spanish, Mexican, and American governors; occupying Pueblo Indians between 1680 and 1692; soldiers (including, briefly, the Texas Confederate Army); a jail; and a post office. In the early 1900s, it was the first headquarters of the School of American Archeology (now the School of American Research), as well as the New Mexico Historical Society. Like the Plaza, the Palace has shrunk over the years; it once stretched north all the way to Paseo de Paralta.

The last two governors to live in the Palace had a lasting impact on New Mexico history. During his 1877–81 tenure, Governor Lew Wallace succeeded in both cleaning up crime by capturing Billy the Kid and writing the biggest-selling novel of its day, *Ben Hur: A Tale of the Christ*. The final territorial governor, Bradford Prince, worked to save the delapidated Palace from demolition in the early 1900s, sparking an architectural renaissance that revolutionized what you see today.

The **Museum of New Mexico** is really four different museums, all of which can be visited Tuesday to Sunday, 10am–5pm; admission is free Friday evenings, 5–8pm. Your best bet is to purchase the $10 Museum of New Mexico pass, valid for four days – one of the city's best deals. New Mexico residents get in for free on Sundays.

The dusty **Museum of New Mexico History** (105 E. Palace Ave, tel: 505/ 476-5100) in the Palace of the Governors itself, is a rabbit warren of a place,

Left: Santa Fe at night
Above: the Plaza. **Right:** market vendors

with thick adobe walls, low wooden ceilings, and small rooms exhibiting permanent exhibits of maps, photographs, portraits of governors, guns, pottery, period furnishings, and the famed Segesser Hides, rare early Spanish paintings on tanned buffalo skin. Look for the 'archeological windows' left behind by recent excavations that reveal earlier uses of the Palace. The Palace's most famous 'exhibit' is a living one: the friendly vendors from New Mexico's 19 pueblos who sell pottery, jewelry, and other crafts beneath the portal each day.

You can find black-on-black pottery from San Ildefonso, redware from Santa Clara, and inlaid jewelry from Zuni, among other items, all authenticated by the museum and reasonably priced. Photography is allowed, but it's good manners to ask first.

There's more art one block west of the Palace at the **Museum of Fine Arts** (107 W. Palace, tel: 505/827-4468), interesting not only for its wonderful collection of New Mexico art but also for its 1917 Pueblo Mission Revival architecture. The building replicates the New Mexico Building commissioned for the Panama-California Exposition in San Diego in 1915, which was inspired by the church at Acoma Pueblo and designed by Trinidad, Colorado, architect Isaac Hamilton Rapp. It was the first building to reflect the new Santa Fe Style following the Palace of the Governors renovation.

MFA concentrates on 20th-century art by New Mexico artists such as Georgia O'Keeffe; the so-called *Cinco Pintores* (Will Shuster, Willard Nash, Fremont Ellis, Walter Mruk, and Josef Bakos); as well as expatriate Taos artists Dorothy Brett and Nicholai Fechin, and others attracted to the state by its combination of cultures, landscape, and light. Of special interest are the murals representing missionary history in the New World painted by Donald

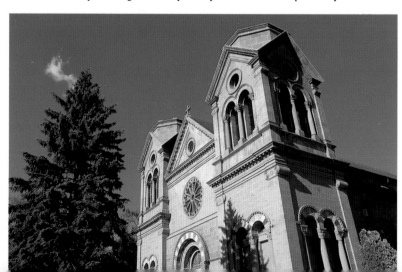

Beauregard and finished by Carlos Vierra and Kenneth Chapman. These can be enjoyed in **St Francis Auditorium**, a popular venue for concerts.

No Santa Fe itinerary is complete without a visit to the **Georgia O'Keeffe Museum** (217 Johnson St, tel: 505/995-0785; same hours as MNM), two blocks west of MFA. The only major museum dedicated to a woman artist in the US, the privately run O'Keeffe Museum opened in July 1997 and was an instant hit. Its 10 simple galleries feature revolving exhibits of O'Keeffe's work between 1916 and 1980. They trace the artist's development from her Wisconsin roots and early Texas teaching career through her creative partnership with her husband, the influential New York photographer Alfred Stieglitz, and eventual move to New Mexico.

Stop for refreshment or lunch at the O'Keeffe Café. The lovely patio comes into its own in summer. Then make your way to Paseo de Peralta, passing many civic buildings. Climb the hill to the **Cross of the Martyrs**, where a cross commemorates the Franciscan priests who were killed during the 1680 Pueblo Revolt that expelled the Spanish from New Mexico for 12 years.

French-born bishop Jean-Baptiste Lamy the subject of Willa Cather's famous novel *Death Comes for the Archbishop*, caused a commotion when he began building **St Francis Cathedral** (213 Cathedral Place; open daily) between 1869 and 1886. In contrast with what one observer called the 'prairie dog town' that surrounded it, this French-Romanesque building was constructed from limestone by master Italian stonemasons and was intended to have two steeples. The new Cathedral was constructed around the 1717 Parroquia, a portion of which can be seen inside the soaring building, along with the oldest Christian religious statue in the country.

La Conquistadora (the Virgin of the Conquest) was carried back to Santa Fe by a triumphant Don Diego de Vargas in 1692. It is a key element in the Mass celebrating Santa Fe's annual September fiesta, a Labor Day Weekend extravaganza commenorating the Reconquest.

Across from the Cathedral is another Santa Fe-style adobe building designed by Isaac Rapp, which until the 1960s housed the main post office. Today, it is home to the **Institute of American Indian Arts Museum** (108 Cathedral Place, tel: 505/983-8900; open Mon–Sat 9am–5pm, Sun noon–5pm). With more than 6,500 pieces representing Indian artists, the museum is the largest repository of contemporary American Indian art in the world and offers a unique opportunity to visit an Indian-run museum.

Entrance to the Institute is through a symbolic Pueblo *kiva*, or ceremonial chamber, then five galleries offer exhibits. A large sculpture garden is dedicated to Allan Houser, the Chiricahua Apache sculptor whose works can

Top left: Museum of Fine Arts. **Left:** St Francis Cathedral
Above: sculpture outside Santa Fe's Georgia O'Keeffe Museum

also be seen in front of the New Mexico Capitol, Hotel Santa Fe, the excellent Wheelwright Museum, and other locations.

Walking south on Cathedral Place, then west of Water Street, you pass another of Bishop Lamy's buildings, the **Loretto Chapel** (211 Old Santa Fe Trail, tel: 505/982-0092; Mon–Sat 9am–6pm, Sun 10:30am–5pm). The first stone masonry building in Santa Fe, the Chapel was built between 1873 and 1878 for the Sisters of Loretto, who taught young women next door at Loretto Academy, now the **Inn at Loretto** *(see pages 21 and 95)*.

The decomissioned Chapel is one of the most beautiful spaces in Santa Fe, frequently used for weddings and concerts. Its focal point is the **Miraculous Staircase**, an apparently unsupported spiral wooden staircase that rises to the choir loft. After the chapel's architect, Lamy's nephew, was killed in a dispute over his affair with a married woman, the chapel was left without a staircase.

According to legend, a stranger arrived, built the staircase, then disappeared without taking payment. The faithful believe it was St Joseph, patron saint of carpenters, but it's now suggested the staircase was really built by a master French carpenter, Francois-Jean Rochas, who moved to a remote local canyon to become a rancher, and took on the task.

Walk back along Old Santa Fe Trail to the southeast corner of the Plaza, which is anchored by **La Fonda**, Santa Fe's most historic hotel. Inns have stood at this spot – the end of both the Santa Fe and earlier El Camino Real trails – for 300 years. In the early 1700s, the Alarid family lived in a large *hacienda* and took in travelers so often their home became known as *la fonda*, the inn. In 1846, the United States Hotel stood here, followed by the Exchange Hotel, a ramshackle affair that can be seen in old photographs.

The last project of Isaac Rapp, the new La Fonda was built in 1920, during the heyday of Southwest tourism that spawned a productive partnership between hotelier Fred Harvey and the railroad. A few years

Top: the Miraculous Staircase, Loretto Chapel
Left: the dining room of La Fonda

later, John Gaw Meem further refined the hotel into a more imposing Pueblo Mission Revival-style structure, complete with belltower, modeled on Taos Pueblo. Thousands of visitors walk through the La Fonda lobby each year. It's a great place to drink in Santa Fe Style décor, do some high-class window shopping, find a restroom, and enjoy free music and dancing nightly in a bar that was once *the* gathering place for Santa Fe's most famous people. **La Plazuela Restaurant**, with its painted glass walls and roof and excellent food, makes an atmospheric (but pricy) place for an early dinner.

End your day by visiting some of the galleries on West Palace and West San Francisco. On Friday nights, you can visit museums for free and attend a number of gallery openings, between 5 and 8pm. West San Francisco Street is a great place for eating and shopping. In the last block, you'll find quaint **Burro Alley**, named for its distinctive donkeys, which stood tied to the rails outside Jake Gold's trading post.

On the corner is the **Lensic Performing Arts Center** *(see pages 84 and 85)*. The Lensic (named using the initials of the previous owner's children) was built in 1931 as a movie palace and is Santa Fe's only example of Mexican Baroque Revival architecture. It occupies the site of an early 19th-century casino run by Doña Tules. She was the most infamous of Santa Fe's liberated women, who shocked newly arrived Americans by 'living in sin', owning businesses, painting her face, smoking cigars, and dancing the Fandango. The Lensic is now the city's premier performing arts venue. Nightly readings, concerts, and other events make the perfect finale to a sojourn in Santa Fe.

2. MUSEUM HILL *(see map, p30)*

Plan on devoting a whole day to these museums. There's ample parking for vehicles, or you can take a 15-minute ride on the 'M' bus, which leaves from the Downtown Sheridan Transit Center, next to the Museum of Fine Arts. You could also walk, combining this tour with part of the Canyon Road itinerary that follows.

Museums don't open until 10am, allowing you time to linger over breakfast. If you're taking the bus, head over to West San Francisco Street, opposite the Lensic, and enjoy New Mexico *huevos* covered in a 'Christmas' – a combination of red and green chile – at **Tia Sophia's** (210 W. San Francisco, tel: 505/983-9880), a longtime favorite haunt. After breakfast, stop in at **Collected Works Bookstore** (208B W. San Francisco, tel: 505/988-4226), to check out local bestsellers and say hello to Kitty Carson, the ginger shop cat. Then cross the street and walk through

Right: *End of the Trail* sculpture, at the entrance to Museum Hill

Burro Alley to the Sheridan Street Transit Center. If you're driving, head over to where St Francis Drive meets Cordova. In the Coronado Shopping Center is the **Santa Fe Baking Company** (504 W. Cordova, tel: 505/988-4292), one of the city's friendliest, most down-home cafés. The super-cheap house special is a Mexican delight.

After breakfast, drive east on Cordova to its junction with Old Pecos Trail. If you have kids, they may be more interested in spending a morning at the

Santa Fe Children's Museum (1050 Old Pecos Trail, tel: 505/989-8359; Wed–Sat 10am–5pm, Sun noon–5pm), one of the few truly kid-oriented places in Santa Fe.

If you're not stopping here, follow the signposts to Museum Hill, off **Old Santa Fe Trail**. The historic trail, in use between 1821 and 1880, entered Santa Fe from the southeast, passing just west of Sun and Moon Mountains. At the entrance to Museum Hill, on Camino Lejo, you'll find the ***End of the Trail*** sculpture, which represents a typical scene during trail days, when Native Americans, Hispanics, and other locals welcomed arriving wagons.

The first museum, on your left, is the **Museum of Spanish Colonial Arts** (750 Camino Lejo, tel: 505/982-2226; Tues–Sat 10am–5pm; admission), housed in a large 1930 Santa Fe-Style residence designed for the director of the Laboratory of Anthropology by architect John Gaw Meem. It is a good place to view *santos*, or depictions of saints, still found in homes. These include *retablos* (paintings on wood and tin) and *bultos* (carved statues), as well as traditional furniture and furnishings, displayed in an intimate home setting.

At the top of the list on Milner Plaza is the **Museum of International Folk Art** (706 Camino Lejo, tel: 505/827-6350; MNM hours), the repository of the world's largest collection of international folk art. Here you'll find 10,000 miniatures from 100 countries displayed in dioramas in the permanent exhibit, while in the Neutrogena Wing are exhibits of textiles, costumes, and masks. The Hispanic Heritage Wing features scale models of adobe homes and Spanish colonial folk art in its *Familia y Fe* exhibit.

Break for a light lunch at the **Museum Café**, where large windows offer views of the Jémez Mountains, then head over to the **Museum of Indian Arts and Culture** (710 Camino Lejo, tel: 505/827-6344; MNM hours). MIAC displays 70,000 prehistoric baskets, pots, textiles, and jewelry collected by archeologist Edgar Lee Hewett, along with other artifacts held in the collections of the Laboratory of Anthropology next door. It's a jewel of a museum, with a stirring multimedia exhibit that tells the stories of the Indians of the Southwest in an accessible, enjoyable way. You can learn about the differences in Pueblo pottery, and enjoy small exhibits on everything from Pueblo textiles to Apache baskets and sculpture in the Lloyd Kiva New Wing, named for a founder of the Institute of American Indian Arts.

Above: exhibit from the Museum of Spanish Colonial Arts
Right: Museum of Indian Arts and Culture

Although it's a little bit tucked away, don't leave without visiting the **Wheelwright Museum of the American Indian** (704 Camino Lejo, tel: 505/982-4636; Mon–Sat 10am–5pm, Sun 1–5pm; free). The product of a partnership between New Englander Mary Cabot Wheelwright and Navajo medicine man Hastiin Klah, the museum was founded in 1937. Its mission was to record the Navajo culture, which was struggling to survive aggressive government policies that sought to integrate Navajos into the mainstream after centuries of traditional herding and farming on their lands. Happily that did not happen, and today the Wheelwright has expanded to include exhibits of contemporary and traditional Southwestern art in a small and atmospheric building designed by Santa Fe artist William Penhallow Henderson. Gifts are available in a replica trading post, and activities include storytelling on summer weekends and a children's powwow in September.

If you have your own vehicle, turn right out of Camino Lejo to enjoy retracing part of Old Santa Fe. If you're a fan of John Gaw Meem's architecture, you'll want to view the **National Park Service – Southwest Office** (1100 Old Santa Fe Trail, tel: 505/988-6100; Mon–Fri 8am–4:30pm; free self-guided tours of the exterior), one of the largest known adobe office complexes in the US. The structure was built by the Civilian Conservation Corps as part of the 1930s New Deal-era Works Progress Administration projects. Young men between 17 and 23 were paid $1 a day to build the structure from 280,000 handmade bricks and to learn traditional woodwork, stone and foundation masonry, and tinwork. Meem also designed the Santa Fe campus of nearby **St John's College**, reached via Camino del Monte Sol.

End your day with dinner at **Harry's Roadhouse** (tel: 805/989-4629) on Old Las Vegas Highway, where Harry and wife Peyton dish up eclectic cuisine at reasonable prices. If you ride the bus back, check out **Coyote Café** (132 W. Water St, tel: 505/983-1615), the restaurant that put Santa Fe on the culinary map. Chef Mark Miller still serves his signature chile-rubbed meats and unique salsas in a lively happening atmosphere. There's cheaper fare on Miller's **Coyote Cantina** rooftop in summer, and downstairs in the **Cottonwoods**, a Southwest diner.

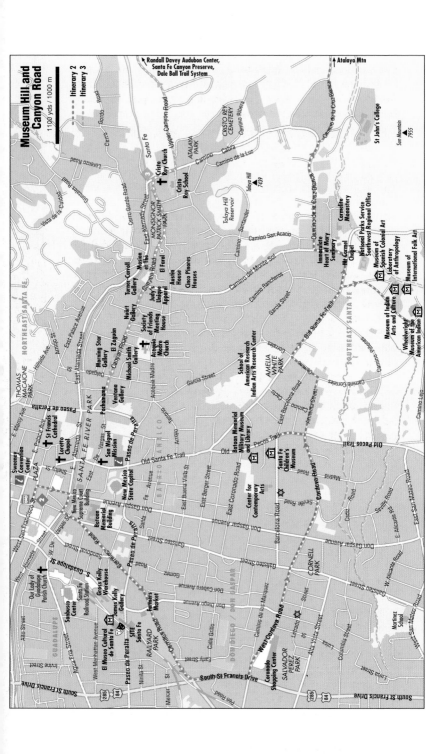

3. CANYON ROAD *(see map, p30)*

This third tour focuses on Santa Fe's famous art district. One of the city's most charming and historic neighborhoods, Canyon Road was used for centuries by Indians and Hispanics as a thoroughfare into the Santa Fe National Forest. Today, a network of trails leave Randall Davey Audubon Center, on Upper Canyon Road – a great place for hiking and birdwatching at any time of year.

Note: This all-day tour can be shortened and combined with the previous Museum Hill tour. Both are accessible via the 'M' bus, which stops on East Alameda, then passes the top of Lower Canyon Road, before continuing to Museum Hill. Or you can walk or drive the mile-long Camino del Monte Sol, which comes out opposite Museum Hill.

Canyon Road winds for 2½ miles (4km) to its terminus in the Santa Fe watershed, but you'll probably find yourself tired if you try to walk it all *and* visit art galleries along the way. One good option is to park (the sidestreets of Garcia and Delgado often have parking available) and view the galleries at the bottom of Lower Canyon Road, then drive up Canyon Road and park in the Municipal Lot at Canyon Road and Camino del Monte Sol, where some of the city's best restaurants are clustered.

There's also parking a little farther up, at **Cristo Rey Church** (1120 Canyon Road, tel: 505/983-8528; daily 7am–7pm; free), one of Santa Fe's most

beautiful Catholic churches. It was designed by John Gaw Meem in 1940 to celebrate the 500th anniversary of the Spanish *Entrada* into New Mexico and features classic local architecture: wide adobe walls, massive ponderosa *viga* ceiling beams interspersed with juniper *latillas*, held up by carved corbel supports atop wooden pillars. The entire church was designed around a massive stone *reredos*, or altar screen, carved by Mexican craftsmen in 1760 for La Castrense, the Mexican military chapel on the Plaza.

When Bishop Lamy arrived in 1859, he hid the altar screen in a side chapel of his new cathedral, where it remained until rescued by Catholic authorities and reinstalled here. The reredos is displayed to best effect in the morning, when light through the eastern clerestory windows falls on the altar, spotlighting the frieze.

For breakfast or lunch, stop in at **The Tea House** (944 Palace, tel: 505/992-0972), in the former Vigil adobe home in **The Stables**, a working artist's compound on Canyon Road. Offering more than 100 custom-blended teas as well

Above: Cristo Rey Church was built in 1940

city itineraries

as some of the lightest, freshest, most inexpensive food in town, this cosmopolitan café is a real find. Here, you can sip a perfectly made cup of tea, share a huge, flaky, homemade apricot-almond scone and whipped cream, and enjoy art from around the world while eavesdropping on conversations in English, Spanish, Portugese, or French. At breakfast, try steamed confetti eggs, feathery eggs steamed with a capuccino machine and served with minced tomatoes, chives, and parmesan. It's delicious.

Canyon Road is the place to be seen in summer, when a cross-section of Santa Fe comes out for well-attended Friday Evening Art Openings. Another local custom is the annual Christmas Eve Farolito Walk, a traditional cele-

bration featuring hundreds of *farolitos,* or brown-bag lanterns symbolically lighting the way for the Christ Child. Many Santa Feans bring guests here to walk the 2-mile (3.2-km) loop, drink hot cider, and warm themselves around bonfires called *luminarias* to the backdrop of carol singing and cries of *'Feliz Navidad!'*

Galleries line both sides of the street for six blocks. The well-known **Turner-Carroll** (725 Canyon) and **Nuärt** (670 Canyon) galleries exhibit contemporary American and European art. Museum-quality American Indian antiques are the specialty at **Michael Smith Gallery** (595 Canyon), which carries extraordinarily beautiful historic Navajo rugs, Pueblo pottery, and other items acquired by trader Michael Smith during his travels. Not far away, contemporary Navajo rugs and other Indian art can be found at **Morningstar Gallery** (513 Canyon Road). **Pachamama** (223 Canyon Road), at the bottom of Canyon Road, is a good place to buy inexpensive tin *milagros*

(literally, miracles), lovely charms that are said to keep the owner safe from harm. **Ventana Gallery** (400 Canyon Road), on the corner of Canyon Road and Garcia, occupies the former Ward School, built in 1906 on the site of a former dance hall. The distinctive brick building, with its turret and Territorial-style trim, is one of a handful of Territorial buildings left in the city.

Starting in the early 1900s, the Canyon Road area became popular with tuberculosis patients from cities back East, seeking a cure in Santa Fe's warm, dry climate. Sunmount Sanitorium (now the Immaculate Heart of Mary Seminary on the corner of Camino del Monte Sol and Old Santa Fe Trail) was designed by I.H. Rapp in 1903 and later expanded by John Gaw Meem, himself a patient there. It didn't attract many clients until 1914, when poet Alice Corbin, writer Mary Austin, photographer Carlos Vierra, Meem, and others began moving to Santa Fe for both creative and health purposes.

These Bohemians built inexpensive adobe homes along Camino del Monte Sol, Canyon Road, Acequia Madre, and other side roads that can still be seen. The oldest artist's residence here is **El Zaguán** (545 Canyon Road), named for its long, enclosed *portal,* typical of northern New Mexico homes. It was

Above: dress up artsy to stroll around Canyon Road

built in 1849 and later bought and expanded by James Johnson, a pioneering Santa Fe Trail trader. It is most famous as one of the Santa Fe homes of Adolph Bandelier, the Swiss archeologist who created the beautiful gardens west of the building. The present owner, Historic Santa Fe Foundation, still rents interior apartments to artists. You can walk inside the compound and look around and also enter the gardens.

Olive Rush, a devout Quaker, was the first woman painter to move to Santa Fe's fledgling art colony, in 1920. All but forgotten now, Rush was an important figure in her day, involved with Dorothy Dunn in encouraging young Indian artists at the Studio at Santa Fe Indian School and painting murals in city buildings as part of the WPA program in the 1930s. Her quaint 1820s adobe home is now the **Society of Friends Meeting House** (630 Canyon Road), which holds weekly meetings open to the public.

Other artist residences can be found on side streets. Gerald Cassidy constructed his unusual home on the corner of Acequia Madre, the street to the south that parallels the Mother Ditch, which still waters gardens. Poet Witter Bynner built a huge adobe residence (the **Inn of the Turquoise Bear**, *see page 96*) off Old Santa Fe Trail and hosted guests like D.H. Lawrence and his wife Frieda in 1922. Mary Austin, author of *Land of Little Rain*, lived at 439 Camino del Monte Sol. Among her neighbors were the clique that called themselves the *Cincos Pintores* (the Five Painters) – Will Shuster, Fremont Ellis, Joseph Bakos, Walter Mruk, and Willard Nash. These artists helped build adobes between 538 and 586 Camino del Monte Sol.

Top: El Zaguán was built in 1849
Right: making a sale

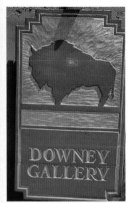

The Cinco Pintores moved to Santa Fe hoping to do apprenticeships with more established artists like William Penhallow Henderson, John Sloan, Gerald Cassidy, and Randall Davey. Davey chose to build his home at the top of what is now Upper Canyon Road, where today it is a scenic part of the huge **Randall Davey Audubon Center** (1800 Upper Canyon Rd, tel: 505/983-4609; daily 9am–5pm; house tours on Mon in summer; admission). One of only a handful of Audubon centers in the US, this delightful spot has a bird-viewing garden, nature exhibits, and an easy trail that ascends to a cool ponderosa pine forest. More than 100 bird species use the pinyon-juniper-clad foothills, some of which can be seen on bird walks offered every Saturday at 8am (9am Nov–Feb).

Trails adjoin those in 190-acre (77-hectare) **Santa Fe Canyon Preserve** (tel: 505/988-3867; daily 7am–7pm; free), now donated to the Nature Conservancy. Opened in April 2002, you can hike trails around a Victorian-era dam and native willow and cottonwood *bosque* bottomlands, and follow the original route of the Santa Fe River. One of the best things is that it links the 25-mile (40-km) **Dale Ball Trail System**, beginning at **Hyde Memorial State Park** (tel: 505/983-7175; just north of Santa Fe off Hyde Park Rd), with 3-mile-long **Atalaya Trail** on the south, which leaves from behind St John's College (*see previous itinerary*).

With all this walking, you'll work up an appetite. For atmosphere alone, **El Farol** (808 Canyon Rd, tel: 505/983-9912), Santa Fe's oldest restaurant, is the sentimental choice. The specialty at El Farol (*farol* is a lantern) is *tapas*, or Spanish appetizers, such as the famous garlic soup, and main courses like paella, served in a dark, wooden-floored adobe with low ceilings. There's live music and dancing most nights, including flamenco onWednesdays. One block west, elegant **Geronimo Restaurant** (724 Canyon Rd, tel: 505/982-1500), located in the 18th-century Borrego House, is a different experience altogether. One of Santa Fe's top 10 restaurants , its specialties include a huge elk tenderloin, ranch-raised in Texas, and a lobster appetizer served with pasta and spicy sauce. It's expensive, but worth every penny. The best deal is lunch, where you'll be able to enjoy the food and atmosphere at a fraction of the cost and still have a chance to walk off the calorie-laden dessert.

4. BARRIO ANALCO *(see map, p18)*

Spend a half-day wandering around Barrio Analco, the oldest neighborhood in Santa Fe, and the New Mexico State Government Complex.

From Santa Fe River Park on East Alameda Street, walk south on Old Santa Fe Trail to East De Vargas Street. Halfway down this tiny alley, you'll find **Jane's** (237 E. De Vargas, tel: 505/983-9894), a café in a converted adobe home with a shady courtyard. London-born Jane serves creative breakfast eggs, quiches, homemade pies, muffins, cookies, and strong French-roast coffee from California. Poetry readings take place here at night.

On the corner of East De Vargas and Old Santa Fe Trail is **San Miguel Mission** (401 Old Santa Fe Trail, tel: 505/983-3974; daily 9am–5pm, Sun to 4pm; admission; audio tours), Santa Fe's oldest church. San Miguel was built between 1610 and 1625 by Tlaxcalan Indians who came as servants to Spanish colonists. Almost destroyed during the 1680 Pueblo Revolt, it was rebuilt in 1710. The wooden *reredos,* or altar screen, installed in 1798, is on display inside along with rare images of Christ painted on buffalo and deer hides and the San Jose Bell, which is thought to date to 1356. The exterior is a favorite with photographers. Its thick buttresses hold up tapered dark brown adobe walls that contrast dramatically with the New Mexico sky.

Across the street, behind Upper Crust Pizza, is the **Oldest House in Santa Fe** (215 E. De Vargas). Swiss archeologist Adolph Bandelier lived at 352 East De Vargas in 1880 and dated the puddled adobe foundations of this dwelling to AD1250, when it was constructed as part of an earlier Indian-pueblo. The rest of the building was built between 1740 and 1767. The interior is a rare example of an 18th-century workman's dwelling, with thick walls, low *viga* beam and *latilla* pole ceilings, dirt floors, and a corner fireplace, known as a *fogon.*

The two brick-and-stucco buildings next to San Miguel Mission – the **Lamy Building** and the fine **Lew Wallace Building** – were constructed in 1878 by the Christian Brothers as part of St Michael's College (now the College of Santa Fe on St Michael's Drive). They are part of the New Mexico State Government Complex. The **Santa Fe Visitors and Convention Bureau** is located here, a good place to stop and pick up free maps and booklets on the city and the state.

The **New Mexico State Capitol** is on the west side of Old Santa Fe Trail. Inspired by the Great Kivas of the ancestors of today's Pueblo Indian people,

Top left: buy art here. **Left:** galleries galore on Canyon Road
Above: San Miguel Mission is Santa Fe's oldest church

the Roundhouse, as it is called, was designed in 1966 by architect W.C. Kruger to resemble the Zia sun symbol on the state flag and seal, with square projections in the four compass directions. In keeping with other state government buildings in the capital complex, the building is designed in the Territorial Revival style, with classic details such as a rotunda, pediments, and white trim.

In 1988, the Roundhouse was retro-fitted to the tune of nearly $29 million, to strip out asbestos in the interior walls. During that time, legislative sessions were held in the adjoining **Bataan Memorial Building** (407 Galisteo St), the old territorial and state capitol. This handsome structure dates from 1900, and was renamed to honor the disproportionate number of victims and survivors from New Mexico's 200th and 515th Coast Artillery Anti-aircraft Regiments in the Philippines who took part in the 1941 Bataan Death March.

The State Capitol is open to the public and free guided tours are offered. Be sure to pick up a guide to the New Mexico art collection on display in and around the Roundhouse. The excellent **Governor's Gallery** upstairs has changing exhibits and occasional receptions. Legislative sessions take place every January and February. House and Senate visitors galleries fill up around 8am, with sessions starting around 10am.

When the Legislature is meeting, parking and reservations at nearby restaurants are at a premium. The colorful characters and buzz of political intrigue make for juicy eavesdropping in popular haunts like the jam-packed **Dragon Bar** at the venerable **Pink Adobe Restaurant** (406 Old Santa Fe Trail, tel: 505/983-7712), opposite San Miguel Mission. The Pink Adobe was founded by artist Rosalie Murphy in the 1940s. Murphy's specialties – the hearty Steak Dunnigan and fragrant green chile-and-chicken Gypsy Stew – still put this place on the map.

5. GUADALUPE–RAILYARDS DISTRICT *(see map, p18)*

Before leaving Santa Fe, make time to spend a few hours touring this historic district, an artsy warehouse area that is rapidly becoming the city's most important community gathering place.

There's no better way of learning about the vital role of sustainable agriculture in preserving New Mexico's vibrant cultures than at the **Santa Fe Farmer's Market** (corner of S. Guadalupe and Cerrillos, tel: 505/983-4098; Tues and Sat 7am–noon), which brings together small-time organic farmers and customers throughout the summer. Get here early and breakfast on piping hot burritos, pastries, and coffee (all profits go to the market), then sample artisan breads, range-fed meats (including bison), hand-crafted goat cheeses, and heritage varieties of squash, tomatoes, and melons. Goat's milk soap, dried flowers, and creative lavender items make unique souvenirs.

There's an openness to the new in the redeveloped Santa Fe Railyards that is now sadly lacking in the high-priced downtown area. Next to the Farmer's Market is SITE **Santa Fe** (1606 Paseo de Peralta, tel: 505/989-1199; Wed–Sun 10am–5pm, Fri to 7pm; admission), a contemporary art gallery housed in an old beer warehouse, which has attracted the likes of environmental artist Andy Goldworthy among other international artists since it opened in 1995.

The **Railyard Performance Center** (1611 Paseo de Peralta, tel: 505/982-8309) offers high-energy dance and music classes, from all-ages marimba groups (who sometimes play at the Farmer's Market) to Saturday morning live-drumming African dance sessions with co-owner Elise Gent. A work-in-progress is **El Museo Cultural** (1615-B Paseo de Peralta, tel: 505/992-0591; Tues–Sun 1–5pm; free). This unusual museum fosters contemporary Hispanic culture by offering workshops, readings, and art exhibits showcasing traditional and modern New Mexico artists. A Winter Farmer's Market is held here on Saturdays from 9am to 1pm between November and May.

The most important building in the Railyards is the 1914 **Gross Kelley Almacen**, an early Spanish Pueblo Mission Revival grocery that's home to several interesting galleries and a restaurant. Gross Kelley faces the 1910 **Atchison, Topeka & Santa Fe Railway Depot**, headquarters for **Santa Fe Southern Railway** (410 S. Guadalupe, tel: 505/989-8600). In the early 1900s, the depot served passengers transferring from the narrow-gauge Denver and Rio Grande Railway 'Chile Line,' linking New Mexico and Colorado, to the branch line of the AT&SF line, whose main depot was in Lamy, southwest of Santa Fe (now the main Amtrak stop for Santa Fe).

Left top: the State Capitol is called 'the Roundhouse.' **Left**: the Pink Abode
Above: locomotive in the Guadalupe-Railyards District

Santa Fe Southern offers popular scenic train rides to Lamy that make a fun excursion, if you have time. Try a Saturday morning ride or a sunset campfire barbecue Friday evenings between April and October.

Old photos show brightly painted 'Chile Line' trains chugging right past **El Santuario de Nuestra Senora de Guadalupe** (100 S. Guadalupe St, tel: 505/988-2027; open daily). This late-1700s church is thought to be the oldest shrine in the US dedicated to the Virgin of Guadalupe, who appeared to a Mexican Indian in the 1500s. El Santuario has been much remodeled (in the mid-1800s, Bishop Lamy converted it to a New England-style church, complete with steeple). Today, it's a museum and concert hall, displaying a 1783 oil painting, *Our Lady of Guadalupe*, and photographs of the building over the years.

The Guadalupe area has shops and restaurants geared toward every budget. The 1880 **Sanbusco Center** (500 Montezuma) has unique shoe and clothing stores and a tiny Salvadoran café for unusual snacks. A typical

night out might include a movie at **Jean Cocteau Cinema** (418 Montezuma, tel: 505/988-2711), which has fresh popcorn with a variety of seasonings, followed by dinner at **Zia Diner** (326 S. Guadalupe, tel: 505/988-7008), an attractive (and affordable) diner in a converted auto shop that offers elegant 'comfort food', from fish & chips to meatloaf and pies. You can find a good bar as well as late-night music at hipper-than-thou **Cowgirl Hall of Fame Bar-B-Q and Western Grill** (319 S.Guadalupe, tel: 505/982-2565) or, a block away, at **The Paramount** (331 Sandoval, tel: 505/982-8999), Santa Fe's best small venue for national touring acts.

Top: where cowgirls go to dine
Left: railroad mural on Guadalupe Street

6. TESUQUE, THE SKI BASIN, AND THE SANTA FE OPERA
(see map, p40)

Drive northeast of Santa Fe into the Sangre de Cristo Mountains, then visit the pretty Hispanic village of Tesuque, a stone's throw from world-famous Santa Fe Opera. Depending on the time of year, you can ski, hike, camp, picnic, horseback ride, visit art galleries, soak in a hot tub, and even glimpse reclusive celebrities whose sprawling adobe estates nestle in the quiet foothills.

Eat breakfast near the Plaza at **The Burrito Company** (111 Washington Ave, tel: 505/982-4453), a Santa Fe favorite for its inexpensive burritos and fast service, then drive north on Washington. As you cross Paseo de Peralta, you can't miss the 1910 **Scottish Rite Temple** on your left. The 'Pink Palace,' as some call it, was designed by California architects Hunt and Burns as an homage to the Alhambra in Spain.

Just past the Temple is **Fort Marcy Recreation Center**, one of several city-run facilities offering a heated indoor swimming pool, fitness and weight machines, and movement classes. Thousands jam the outdoor stadium every Labor Day Weekend for the Burning of Zozobra, a 44-ft- (13-m-) high puppet representing Old Man Gloom. The ceremony was the brainchild of eccentric artist Will Shuster. Shuster invented the pagan ritual in the 1920s as one of several community events during Fiesta, the traditional reenactment of the Reconquest of New Mexico.

Across from Fort Marcy is **Artist Road**, the beginning of the 16-mile (26-km) scenic byway to **Santa Fe Ski Basin** (tel: 505/982-4429), which each winter attracts 3,500 downhill and crosscountry skiers a day on 43 trails. The narrow, winding road climbs out of the pinyon-juniper zone into ponderosa pine and Gambel oak forest, then into one of the West's largest aspen groves, and finally reaches mixed spruce-fir conifers growing at the ski basin with its 10,000-ft (3,000-m) elevation. Early October is the peak time for this 1½-hour round-trip. Changing oaks and aspens splash brilliant colors across the mountainsides and make a hike into the forest or a ride in the ski lift a photographer's dream.

On the 6-mile (10-km) **Big Tesuque Creek Trail**, watch for mule deer and bright-blue Steller's and pinyon jays. Make lots of noise in early fall to deter black bears, sometimes seen at dusk fattening up on acorns for the long winter ahead. Wear hiking boots, a hat, layered clothes, high SPF sunscreen, and carry nutritious snacks. Drink a gallon of water per day to avoid dehydration at this elevation.

If you make a day of it, consider stopping at world-famous **Ten Thousand Waves** (3451 Hyde Park Rd, tel: 505/982-9304) as you drive back down the mountain at sunset. This Japanese health spa

Right: Ten Thousand Waves Japanese spa

offers outdoor hot tubs (including a cheaper communal tub), Santa Fe's best massages, and cabins for rent, all in an aesthetically pleasing forest setting.

Back at Fort Marcy, Washington Street becomes Bishop's Lodge Road as it heads toward Tesuque past the **Governor's Mansion**, on the left, and discreet homes in the hills. About 5 miles (8km) from the Plaza, on the right, is **Bishop's Lodge Resort and Spa** (tel: 505/983-6377), a good place for food. Once the private retreat of Bishop Lamy, the Bishop's Lodge, which adjoins Pecos Wilderness on the east, has been operating as a resort since 1918. This is a great place for horseback riding and getting away from it all.

Drive slowly through the woodsy village of **Tesuque** and stop at **Shidoni Foundry and Gallery** (tel: 505/988-8001). Wander the 8-acre (3-hectare) sculpture garden, and if you're here on a Saturday afternoon, watch bronzes being poured in the foundry. It's a fascinating experience – one that will make your visit to Santa Fe particularly memorable. There are two good eating places in downtown Tesuque. **El Nido** (CR 73 at Bishops Lodge Rd, tel: 505/988-4340) occupies a former dance hall and trading post and has somewhat pricy fish, meat, and local specialties. Across the street, **Tesuque Village Market** (tel: 505/988-8848) is a great place to stop anytime for takeout coffee, baked goods, and sit-down meals. In summer, it's a popular stop for gourmet fixings for 'tailgate picnics' at the opera, which is just on the other side of US 84/285.

Even if you haven't got a clue about opera, a visit to the **Santa Fe Opera** (tel: 800/280-4654) is fascinating. Perched on a hillside, next to Tesuque Pueblo, the 2,128-seat open-air theater commands panoramic views of the Jémez and Sangre de Cristo Mountains. The 600-member company has mounted more than 130 operas to date, including nine world premieres. Five operas are presented each summer, starting in July, and typically include such favorites as Strauss, Verdi, and Mozart, as well as new works. Tickets go fast, but standing-room is often available. Backstage tours are offered daily.

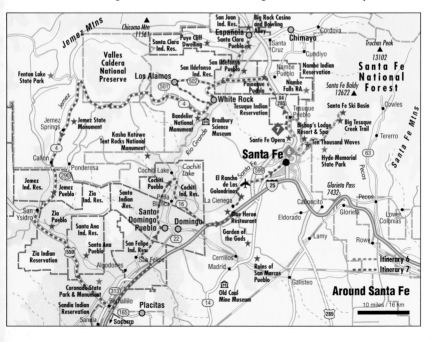

7. SANTA FE AREA PUEBLOS AND
THE JEMEZ MOUNTAINS *(see map, p40)*

There's lots to see and do on this 150-mile (240-km) scenic weekend tour of the Jémez Mountains, west of Santa Fe. Among the attractions are ancient and contemporary Indian pueblos, the birthplace of the atom bomb, national and state parks, and rustic hot springs.

Begin your morning by eating in Santa Fe or at Tesuque Village Market in the Hispanic village of Tesuque, off US 285/84 *(see previous itinerary)*. Then return to the highway and start driving north. Just ahead, west of the highway, is **Tesuque Pueblo** (tel: 505/983-2667), a conservative Indian pueblo that holds 17,000 acres (6,900 hectares) of irrigated lands near the Rio Grande as well as ponderosa pine high country in Santa Fe National Forest. Most of Tesuque Pueblo's visitor attractions lie on either side of the highway, where the tribe operates the popular **Tesuque Flea Market**, **Camel Rock Campground**, and **Casino**, named for the distinctive rock formation nearby. This pueblo is known for its brightly painted ceramic rain-god figurines, which were popular curios during the early 1900s. These are now being revived by Tesuque artists but are still hard to find. On Christmas Day, this quiet, private pueblo holds its winter dances honoring sacred animals.

Continue directly to **Pojoaque Pueblo** (tel: 505/455-3460), a pueblo that is geared toward tourists. Pojoaque (pronounced Po-Wo-Kay) operates a Tourist Information Center, a shopping center, restaurants, a hotel, a casino, a gas station,

Top: Bandelier Loop Trail
Right: take a road trip to the mountains

and the 36-hole **Towa Golf Course**. Although it appears modern, this pueblo remains rooted in the past. It is reintroducing bison on its lands and encourages potters, painters, sculptors, and weavers. Art classes are offered at the **Poeh Cultural Center**, modeled after an ancestral pueblo. Pojoaque's feast day is December 12, a day it shares with the Virgin of Guadalupe, the Black Madonna, revered in New Mexico.

US 502 heads west into the Jémez Mountains along the southern margin of **Española Valley**. To the north are prominent badlands known as *Las Barrancas*, a series of pinkish eroded rocks where paleontologists have found skeletons of extinct southwestern camels.

Any of the turnoffs here offer an interesting backway through tiny Hispanic land-grant villages wedged into Indian lands in the shadow of **Black Mesa**, an isolated volcanic promontory east of the Rio Grande. Pueblos in the Española Valley consider Black Mesa sacred, especially **San Ildefonso Pueblo** (tel: 505/455-3549), whose residents barricaded themselves atop the mesa in 1694 to protest the Reconquest of New Mexico.

The ancestors of today's residents of San Ildefonso moved from Bandelier National Monument during the 1300s, following a long drought. This ancestral link bore unexpected fruit in 1919, when archeologist Edgar Lee Hewett shared examples of the pottery he was uncovering on the Pajarito Plateau with San Ildefonso elder Julian Martínez and his potter wife María. The Martínezes, and later their son Popovi Da and grandson Tony Da, revived the subtle black-on-black pottery that is now a hallmark of the pueblo. It is found in major collections throughout the world. The pueblo museum has examples of María's work, and a number of small, family-owned shops sell pottery as well

as paintings, embroidery, moccasins, and silver jewelry. Dances take place on San Ildefonso's enormous plaza throughout the year, including the evocative Christmas Day Buffalo Dance and feast day celebration on January 23.

Black-on-black pottery, as well as polished redware, is also found at adjoining **Santa Clara Pueblo** (tel: 505/753-7330), which you can visit by crossing the Rio Grande via Otowi Bridge and turning north on NM 30. With 2,600 residents, Santa Clara is the second largest of New Mexico's so-called Eight Northern Pueblos, with 50,000 acres (20,000 hectares) of land. The most extraordinary thing about Santa Clara is that its ancestral home is nearby, in the lower reaches of the Pajarito ('little bird') Plateau. At present, **Puye Cliff Dwellings** historical site is closed to the public, after 700 acres (280 hectares) of pueblo land were damaged by fire in the year 2000, but you are welcome to explore the 'modern' pueblo, which was founded in the 1400s, and visit galleries run by well-known potters such as the Naranjo family.

Santa Clara Pueblo owns **Big Rock Casino and Bowling Alley** in neighboring **Española**. If you come this far, you might want to stop for lunch in the excellent little restaurant adjoining the casino, which serves up inexpensive New Mexican dishes in a no-frills setting. If you stay on US 502, eat in Los Alamos. The **Hill Diner** (1315 Trinity Drive, tel: 505/662-9745) is a good bet for burgers, fries, and other All-American fare.

When Manhattan Project leaders Robert Oppenheimer and General Leslie Groves visited the Pajarito Plateau near **Los Alamos** in the fall of 1942, this mesa had been used for more than 20 years as Los Alamos Ranch School, an academy where well-to-do boys studied the classics and received an outdoor

education. Beginning in April 1943, the government took over the facility, installing scientists who raced to beat Germany in developing the atomic bomb. You can learn more about the top-secret Manhattan Project at the **Bradbury Science Museum** (15th and Central, tel: 505/667-4444; Tues–Fri 9am–5pm, Sat–Sun 1–5pm; free).

If you're short on time, I'd suggest skipping Los Alamos and proceeding to **Bandelier National Monument** (off NM 4, tel: 505/672-3861; open daily; admission), which in the 1100s and 1200s became the center of an important new pueblo civilization. The people who founded new villages on the 300-mile-long (482-km) Pajarito Plateau were refugees from the powerful Chaco culture.

Chaco collapsed dramatically in the early 1100s, probably due to a long drought, and Chacoans were forced into surrounding mountains to begin life anew. Many families walked southeast into the Valles Caldera, the collapsed midsection of the volcanic Jémez Mountains, which had long been a

Left top: Pojoaque Pueblo. **Left:** visitors to the Poeh Cultural Center
Right: J.R. Oppenheimer in an exhibit at the science museum in Los Alamos

traditional pilgrimage spot for collecting obsidian for arrowheads and tools. They eventually put down roots amid the well-watered canyons and mesas carved by tributaries of the Rio Grande on the eastern side of the mountains.

In **Frijoles Canyon**, the heart of Bandelier National Monument, residents farmed the fertile banks of the year-round Frijoles River and built ingenious south-facing cave homes by scooping out the soft volcanic tuff in the nearby cliffs. Deer, elk, rabbits, and other game were plentiful. So were wild plants, such as pinyon nuts, one of the most important crops in the Southwest. People began to relax, and creativity flowed. Women even began making their distinctive black-and-white pottery again.

If you only visit one national park while in northern New Mexico, make it Bandelier. Highlights along the **Main Loop Trail** through Frijoles Canyon

include Long House, Alcove House, and other cave-like homes in the cliffs; 13th-century Tyuonyi Pueblo; and Ceremonial Cave, located at the top of three very steep ladders 150ft (46m) above the canyon floor. More than 2,600 archeological sites have been found in Bandelier, most in the 75 percent protected as wilderness. Seventy miles (110km) of trails make this a great place for hiking. One of the best day hikes is **Falls Trail**, which descends to the Rio Grande to two waterfalls, passing a rare *maar* (steam-born volcano).

Bandelier National Monument was set aside in 1916. Most of its charming wooden visitor buildings date to the 1930s, when they were built by members of the Civilian Conservation Corps (CCC), a government-sponsored Works Progress Administration (WPA) project. The park is named in honor of Swiss-born archeologist Adolph Bandelier, who explored most of New Mexico on foot in the 1880s. Bandelier, the Father of New Mexico archeology, was led here by a guide from Cochiti Pueblo, whose members make regular pilgrimages to the park today.

If you're spending the night in the Jémez Mountains, don't leave Bandelier too late. NM 4 is a narrow, winding mountain road, best driven in daylight hours. If you enjoy camping, stay in the park, where you'll find attractive campsites in two campgrounds amid the ponderosa pine forests above Frijoles Canyon. Otherwise, continue on NM 4, which skirts **Valles Caldera National Preserve** (tel: 505/661-3333), an extraordinary new natural area set aside to protect Valles Caldera, at 14 miles (22km) long, one of the largest collapsed volcano calderas in the world.

Roadside interpretive signs tell the story of the volcanic activity that led

Above: a Long House dwelling in Bandelier National Park

to the explosion, more than a million years ago, that created the Jémez Mountains. The preserve is open for limited hiking, fishing, hunting, and wagon rides, by reservation; call for information.

Redondo Peak in Valles Caldera remains sacred to the people of Jémez Pueblo who migrated into the nearby Jémez Springs area from the vicinity of Mesa Verde in the 1100s. They built multistory pueblos on the mesa tops of San Diego Canyon, but by the early 1600s, European diseases and warfare had decimated the population.

The survivors coalesced into two pueblos: Guisewa in Jémez Springs and Walatowa, a few miles to the south. By 1630, even Guisewa had been abandoned, leaving only a handful of people at Walatowa.

Guisewa is now protected as **Jémez State Monument** (NM 4, tel: 505/829-3530; daily 8am–5pm; admission), at the north end of **Jémez Springs**. This tiny rustic resort community, in the heart of San Diego Canyon, is the perfect place to spend the night. Folks come from far away to soak in the piped hot springs at the 1870s **Jémez Bath House** (Jémez Springs Plaza, tel: 505/829-3303; daily 10am–7:30pm, extended summer hours), which is city run and has private bath tubs and massage rooms. Everything in Jémez Springs is clustered together, so park and walk.

Next to Jémez State Monument is **Los Ojos Restaurant and Saloon** (tel: 505/829-3547), a smoky roadhouse with plenty of evening atmosphere and live music. You'll find several country-charming bed-and-breakfasts in Jémez Springs, where you can fall asleep lulled by the burble of the Jémez River.

The three log cabins for rent at **Giggling Star** (tel: 505/829-3410) are nothing fancy but the inn does have its own riverside hot springs – a big plus.

Next morning, explore Jémez State Monument. The ruined 1622 Spanish mission church dominates the scene here, with its wonderful adjoining *convento* and cloisters.

The unexcavated remains of the large farming pueblo of Guisewa (which once sprawled all the way to the river) are now buried beneath hummocks, and only a restored great *kiva* hints at their importance. The small museum has excellent interpretive exhibits, incor-

Top: cave dwellings, Bandelier National Park
Right: mission ruins, Jémez State Monument

around santa fe

porating the viewpoints of archeologists and the Jémez Tribe. Kids will enjoy touching the reproduction turkey-feather blankets, and grinding corn.

The museum's highlight is its rare Jémez black-on-white pottery, a style of ceramics abandoned as a protest against the Spanish Reconquest when the remaining tribespeople moved to Walotowa Pueblo in 1706. Later generations of Jémez potters made a completely different kind of pottery that resembled the black-on-red and black-on-tan ware made by their neighbors at Zia Pueblo. **Jémez Pueblo** is graced with several well-known artists and writers, including Pulitzer Prize-winning author N. Scott Momaday and Cliff Fragua, whose white marble sculpture of Popé, a leader of the Pueblo Revolt, is one of two statues representing New Mexico in the US Capitol.

Jémez is a closed pueblo, only open on the Feast Day of San Diego on November 12 and for holiday dances. Its main contact with the public is at the recently opened **Walatowa Visitor Center** (7413 NM 4, tel: 505/834-7235; open daily), amid the glorious red rocks of Walatowa. The small facility has exhibits on the area's geology and natural and cultural history, a museum, information on the Jémez Mountains, pottery displays, and a nature trail. If you have time, consider taking one of the tribe's day-long cultural tours and fishing trips on reservation land.

Santa Ana Pueblo (tel: 505/867-3301), just east of tiny Zia Pueblo, is one of New Mexico's most visible tribes. Its thriving businesses line US 550 in Bernalillo and include the **Santa Ana Star Casino**, a championship golf course where you can dine on gourmet fare at Prairie Star restaurant, and a wholesale agriculture business specializing in organic produce. Elements of all these endeavors are incorporated into the pueblo's star attraction, the 500-acre (200-hectare) **Hyatt Regency Tamaya Resort and Spa**, the first luxury resort on Indian land in northern New Mexico. Guests can play golf, walk with a naturalist along a restored cottonwood *bosque* along the Rio Grande, tour sacred lands on horseback, relax in a full-service spa featuring native-inspired products, take a balloon ride and dine in the outstanding Corn Maiden restaurant.

Santa Ana artisans are renowned for their crosses of inlaid straw and polished polychrome pottery, which were revived several decades ago to great acclaim. These and other artworks adorn every room of the hotel, whose circular, multi-story layout evokes the overscaled pueblo architecture of Chaco Canyon. The ancestral pueblo of **Tamaya**, 9 miles (14km) away, is closed to visitors except on feast days, but the hotel has an excellent little cultural center, where you can learn about history and customs from a tribal member.

From here, continue into Albuquerque *(see page 74)*, or return to Santa Fe on Interstate 25, following the former route of historic **Route 66**. En

Top: the Santa Ana Star Casino is one of 10 Indian-run gaming houses in New Mexico

route, you'll pass several more pueblos. **San Felipe Pueblo** (tel: 505/876-3381) was founded in 1706 and is nestled against the West Bank of the Rio Grande beneath Black Mesa. The tribe runs the popular **Hollywood Casino** east of the interstate. San Felipe's lands adjoin those of **Santo Domingo Pueblo** (tel: 505/465-2214), one of New Mexico's largest pueblos, with 2,000 registered members. Highly traditional Santo Domingo is known for its *heishi,* a type of turquoise jewelry once used as currency, and huge Corn Dances, held on its feast day in August and in Christmas week. The tribe runs a small arts and crafts center and a discount gas station, which has the best prices in northern New Mexico.

Cochiti Pueblo (tel: 505/465-2244) is off the beaten track, situated in the volanic country to the west of La Bajada incline, not far from its ancestral home of Bandelier. The focal point is the 1598 **San Buenaventura de Cochiti Church**, which hosts the tribe's feast day ceremonies on July 14. Cochiti is well known for its ceremonial drums and storyteller ceramic figurines, which were popularized by Helen Cordero in the 1960s. **Kasha Katuwe Tent Rocks National Monument** (daily 7am–6pm; free) is located on 4,100 acres (1,660 hectares) of land sacred to the Cochiti. The main trail winds among eerie minaret-shaped cones of pale volcanic tuff that settled here following the creation of the Jémez Mountains. A more strenuous trail climbs onto the mesa top and has panoramic views.

If you're driving back to Santa Fe early enough in the day, make a detour to the tiny village of **La Cienega**, 15 miles (24km) southwest of Santa Fe. To reach it, get off the interstate at exit 276 and bear right on NM 599, the relief route that bypasses Santa Fe. Turn left immediately onto the frontage road and right just before the racetrack on Los Pinos Road. About 3 miles (5km) from the intersection is **El Rancho de los Golondrinas** (tel: 505/471-2261), a living-history ranch on a 1710 Spanish land grant. Dozens of his-

toric cabins, grist mills, churches, *haciendas*, and other buildings have been reconstructed here. They are staffed with costumed interpreters Wednesday to Sunday between April and October. As you wander around on a self-guided tour, see demonstrations of wool dying, sheep shearing, blacksmithing, baking in a bee-hive oven, and other Spanish-colonial activities.

End the day with a fabulous (and reasonably priced) meal in the calm, Zen-like atmosphere of the **Blue Heron Restaurant** at **Sunrise Springs Resort**, a retreat center with lovely shady grounds just before you reach El Rancho de las Golondrinas.

Right: exploring the Indian lands of the Hyatt Regency Tamaya Resort

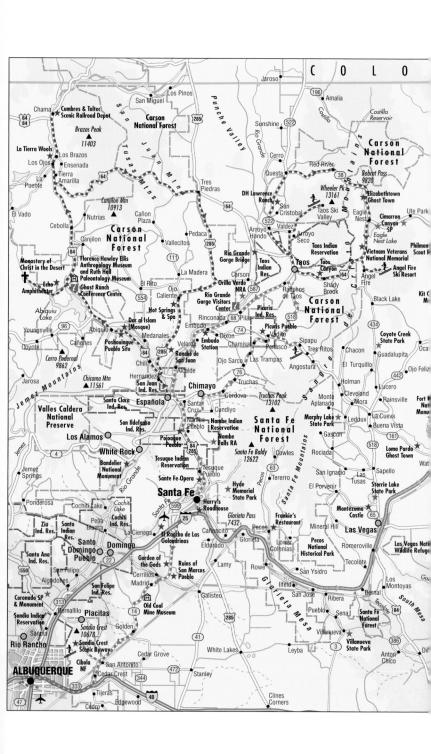

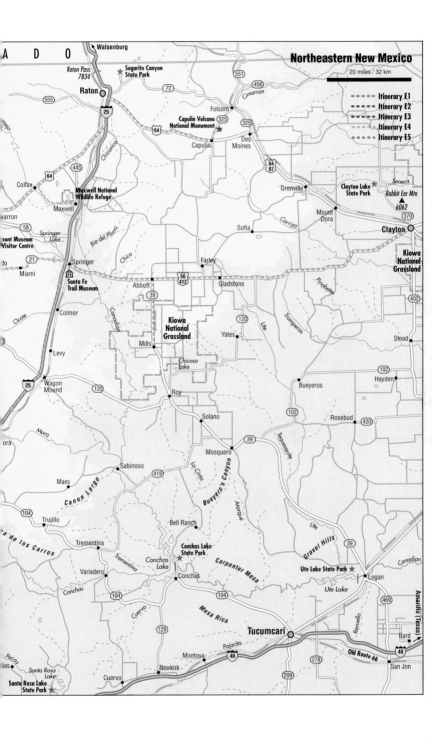

Northeastern New Mexico

20 miles / 32 km

Itinerary E1
Itinerary E2
Itinerary E3
Itinerary E4
Itinerary E5

excursions

Excursions

1. THE HIGH ROAD TO TAOS *(see map, p48)*

This overnight excursion into the Sangre de Cristo Mountains, northeast of Santa Fe, is best done the last two weekends in September, when fall color and the annual 100-studio High Road Art Tour (tel: 505/351-1078) make for a highly photogenic outing. Return via the scenic Rio Grande Gorge, or continue to Taos for one to two nights.

I suggest driving to **Chimayó** in the afternoon and spending the night at **Rancho Manzana** (tel: 888/505-2277), a reasonably priced bed-and-breakfast housed in the beautifully restored former Ortega family mercantile on Chimayó's historic **Plaza del Cerro**, dating from 1740. Chimayó is a half-hour's drive from Santa Fe, via US 285/84. Turn right on NM 503, just past Pojoaque, continue through Nambe, and then make a left on NM 520 into Chimayó valley.

Chimayó is made up of several interconnected neighborhoods, or *placitas*, built in the early 1700s. Hispanic farmers returning to the area following the Pueblo Revolt were offered a land grant on condition they build their homes close together around defensible, pueblo-style plazas that protected the inhabitants from Comanche and Apache raiders. The town is famous for its weavers. Generations of Trujillos and Ortegas have perfected the art of weaving, developing a variant of the Rio Grande style, using wool from hardy Spanish churro sheep and designs that emphasize bright stripes and diamond patterns. **Ortega's Weaving Shop** (tel: 505/351-4215), at the junction of NM 520 and 76, a short walk from Plaza del Cerro, has been in business since 1900 and has fine demonstrations of the craft.

Another old Ortega home on Plaza del Cerro houses the **Chimayó Museum** (tel: 505/351-0945; call for hours). This delightful community museum is a good first stop for visitors. It has exhibits on village history and information on walking tours. You may even meet Don Usner, a member of the Ortega family, who has written extensively about Chimayó.

Chimayó Museum's main mission is to preserve local culture. It recently partnered with the nonprofit Trust for Public Lands to buy historic family-owned pastures, or *potreros*, to keep them in traditional use. One such *potrero* is behind **El Santuario de Nuestro Señor de Esquipulas,** the famous religious shrine that has been dubbed the 'Lourdes of America.' Some 300,000 people a year visit

Left: on the road in New Mexico
Right: making a note of the cowgirl

this former family chapel on the south end of the village. Most come during Easter, when Catholics from all over New Mexico make the pilgrimage on foot, some carrying crosses. They've been coming since 1814, when a priest built a shrine around a well of soil in which a cross kept miraculously appearing.

A tiny room now houses *El Pozo*, the holy well. Visitors purchase candles and bags for sacred dirt at nearby stores. Many return to the shrine with testaments of healing and leave shoes, photos, crutches, and other items in front of a statue of Santo Niño de Atocha, the Spanish child saint reputed to wear out his shoes nightly helping poor villagers. The original cross, displaying the Black Christ of Guatemala, now sits on the altar of the adjoining adobe chapel backed by a beautiful carved wood *reredos*, or altar screen, created by the celebrated 19th-century *santero* known as Molero. No matter what your faith, a visit to this profoundly spiritual sanctuary will fill you with a lasting peace. This is my favorite destination in all of northern New Mexico.

Chimayó's other claim to fame is its wonderful chile, which ripens slightly later than Hatch chile in southern New Mexico. You can buy it green, but it is best ripened on strings known as *ristras*, then ground, which brings out its sweet, complex wine-like flavor. Cooks will kiss you if you bring them ground Chimayó chile; buy a bag of it and other souvenirs next to the Santuario, at **El Potrero Trading Post**.

For dinner, you might try the red-chile-marinaded pork dish, *carne adovada*, a specialty at **Rancho de Chimayó** (tel: 505/351-0444). This wildly popular restaurant is a favorite with out-of-towners. It's run by the Jaramillo family

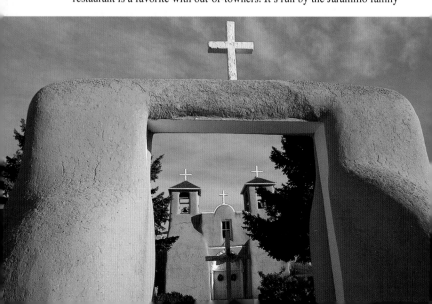

in their old hacienda, located between the Santuario and Plaza de Cerro.

The High Road proper begins at the junction of NM 76, on the north end of Chimayó. First stop is the village of **Cordova**, renowned for its wood-carving, and **San Antonio de Padua Church**. The road then winds onto a broad 8,000-ft (2,400-m) plateau at **Truchas**, named for the trout that are often pulled from crystal-clear mountain streams. Magnificent panoramic views take in 13,102-ft- (3,994-m-) high **Truchas Peak**, the state's second-highest summit, as well as the Rio Grande Valley, Jémez Mountains, and San-dia Mountains. Truchas was founded in 1754 by a dozen families from Chimayó and is also built around a defensible plaza. Art is a big part of town life. Famed *santero* Pedro Antonio Fresquis, known as the Truchas Mas-ter, lived here in the 1700s. You may recognize Truchas from Robert Red-ford's 1987 film adaptation of John Nichols's well-known novel *The Milagro Beanfield War*. Views from here are breathtaking.

Aspens that change color, north of Truchas, make this part of the drive spectacular in the fall. You'll find numerous spots to pull off and hike. Car-son National Forest Ranger Station (tel: 505/587-2255), up ahead in **Peñasco**, has information on hiking, camping, and other activities. They can also tell you about skiing at **Sipapu Ski Area**, a popular destination with Taos ski-iers, just east of Peñasco off NM 518.

Before you get to Peñasco, you'll pass through **Las Trampas** (the Traps), another land-grant settlement founded by families from Santa Fe in 1751. This quiet village has one major attraction: **San José de Gracía Church**, one of the best examples of monumental adobe mission architecture still standing. To see the inte-rior, inquire at La Tiendita, a little store oppo-site the church.

Another church worth seeing is the restored 18th-century **San Lorenzo de Picurís Church** at **Picurís Pueblo** (tel: 505/587-2519), the smallest and most remote of the Rio Grande pueblos. Stop at **Picurís Pueblo Museum** (tel: 505/587-2957) to pick up per-mits to tour the village and take photos. On sale are the tribe's micaceous pottery, weav-ing, and beadwork. Picurís raises bison for sale to the public and for use in the tribally owned **Hotel Santa Fe**. Get to Picurís Pueblo by driving west on NM 75, just before Peñasco, and following signs.

After the NM 518 turnoff at Peñasco, it's only a few miles to **Ranchos de Taos**, the southernmost community of Taos. Taos Indian farmers founded this small community, which is today a quiet, artsy roadside village with several good galleries and restaurants. It's best known for the **San Francisco de Asís Church** (1730) on its old plaza. The enor-mous buttresses and adobe walls in the back of the church have inspired

Top left: a symbol of the Southwest. **Left:** San Francisco de Asís Church
Right: interior of El Santuario de Nuestro Señor de Esquipulas

numerous artists, including photographer Ansel Adams and painter Georgia O'Keeffe, both of whom rendered the church many times in their careers. Visit the church, then stop for lunch at the **Trading Post Café**. This is one of the best restaurants around, but you don't have to order fancy fare.

If you're not continuing to Taos, turn left on NM 68 and return to Santa Fe via the **Rio Grande Gorge**, where the river flows within a narrow, volcanic canyon. This part of the river was set aside as a park in 1959 and became popular with river runners attracted by the state's best whitewater; it is now known as the **Orilla Verde National Recreation Area**. In **Pilar** is the **Rio Grande Visitor Center** (tel: 505/751-4899). You'll find put-ins and takeouts for daylong river-rafting trips nearby. Many companies in Santa Fe offer river trips; call the BLM at 505/757-8851 for a list. Remember to add an extra day to this itinerary if you wish to run the river.

If you decide to stay another night, I suggest heading to historic **Embudo Station** (tel: 800/852-4707). Housed in the remains of the last narrow-gauge railroad station on the Chile Line between Colorado and Santa Fe, this popular spot on the Rio Grande has everything a visitor could want: a restaurant serving quick burger-type lunches and elegant dinners, a microbrewery producing 24 ales (including a popular, spicy green-chile beer), a winery, and an organic garden. You can also spend the night in a small cabin.

In addition to growing their own produce and flowers, the owners buy them from their neighbors the Campos family, whose organic farm is about a mile away. You can rent *casitas* (cottages) on the property and help the family harvest onions, broccoli, garlic, and other crops. The Campos also offer Comida de Campos (tel: 505/852-0017), cooking classes in which guests learn about traditional New Mexican cuisine using an outdoor clay oven, or *horno*.

There's no shortage of good things to eat in this area. Apples are the main crop in Embudo and nearby **Velarde** is known for its quaint fruit stands. In **Dixon**, east of Embudo on NM 75, you'll find art studios and **Chiripada Winery** (NM 75, Dixon, tel: 505/579-4437). From here, you're about an hour from Santa Fe, but drive carefully after dark on the narrow gorge road.

Top: the Rio Grande Gorge has the best white-water rafting in New Mexico

2. THE TOWN OF TAOS AND THE ENCHANTED CIRCLE
(see maps, p48 and p56)

An hour and a half north of Santa Fe, Taos (pop. 6,000) has a long history of attracting creative, idiosyncratic people, including socialites like Mabel Dodge Luhan and Millicent Rogers, mountain man Kit Carson, writer D.H. Lawrence, and artists who founded the state's first art colony in 1898. Give yourself plenty of time – preferably a long weekend – to soak up the artsy mountain-town atmosphere, which many people say is how Santa Fe used to be before it 'sold out.'

One of the best ways to immerse yourself in Taos's free-spirited culture is to stay at the **Mabel Dodge Luhan House** (240 Morada Lane, tel: 800/846-2235), a bed-and-breakfast inn housed in the Pueblo-style home built in 1918 by arts patron Mabel Dodge Luhan and her Taos Pueblo husband Tony Luhan. This isn't just a B&B; it's an experience. You'll stay in simple, elegant, Southwest-style rooms that once hosted Georgia O'Keeffe, Robinson Jeffers, Ansel Adams, and other famous creatives.

Mabel's over-the-top personality is everywhere, particularly in her old quarters in the glassed-in conservatory on top of the house, where you can sleep in her ornately carved bed and bathe in an old-fashioned bathroom with windows painted by D.H. Lawrence. This inn is the perfect choice if you're traveling solo and are interested in meeting kindred spirits. Workshops focusing on meditation, writing, and the arts are hosted regularly here, and you'll find yourself having long, fascinating discussions over breakfast, which would surely meet with the approval of the inn's former owner.

The compact historic downtown area, on either side of Pueblo del Norte, is just a block away, so you'll be able to walk everywhere. A half a block west is the **Kit Carson Home and Museum** (Kit Carson Rd, tel: 505/758-0505; Apr–Oct daily 9am–5pm; admission), the former residence of one of the West's most famous mountain men. Carson first came west from Missouri on the Santa Fe Trail in 1826, pursuing a rugged life in the mountains as a trapper, scout, translator, and eventually army officer dealing with the 'Indian problem,' his most controversial role.

In 1843, Carson bought these four modest rooms as a wedding present for his young bride María Josefa Jaramillo. After both Carsons died suddenly in 1868, their belongings were sold to care for their seven children, so much of what is seen today are furnishings of the period. Exhibits interpret Carson's unexpected rise to fame. One room has guns from the period; another showcases a Trapper's Hall of Fame. Kids will enjoy the walk-through mountain man's camp.

Right: lonesome blues no more

Carson and fellow mountain men Ceran St Vrain and Charles Bent founded Taos's first freemason brotherhood in the mid-1800s. By then, Ceran St Vrain had moved to Taos and opened a store on the south side of the historic **Plaza**. The former mercantile is now the **La Fonda Hotel**, home to Joseph's Table, arguably Taos's best new restaurant, which sits amid a sea of restaurants, galleries, and T-shirt stores. The hotel lobby displays the owner's collection of D.H. Lawrence paintings, which are not very inspiring.

Bent was installed as the first US governor of New Mexico in 1846, after the United States seized the state from Mexico. The following year, he and other Americans were murdered by a group of Hispanic settlers and Taos Indians in a three-week uprising. The **Bent Home and Museum** (tel: 505/758-2376; daily 10am–5pm) is just across Paseo del Norte, at 117 Bent Street, and is open to visitors. Opposite is **Bent Street Grill**, where you can join the locals for tasty snacks, then wander next door to **Moby Dickens Bookstore** to learn more about Lawrence's stay in New Mexico from its well-informed owner.

Interesting art museums are located in historic adobe buildings along **Ledoux Street**, about a half-mile south of the Plaza, off Camino de la Placita. One of the first buildings is the Taos gallery of famed contemporary Navajo artist R.C. Gorman, whose stylized art of Native women is very recognizable. A few doors down is the **E.L. Blumenschein Home and Museum** (222 Ledoux St, tel: 505/758-0505; daily 9am–5pm; admission). A typical adobe with rooms dating to 1797, this cool building is the former home of early 20th-century artist Ernest Blumenschein who, along with Bert Phillips, founded the Taos Society of Artists.

As the story goes, the two New York artists were traveling in New Mexico on a sketching trip in 1898, when their wagon wheel broke in Taos Canyon and they were forced to stay in town to get it repaired. Both men fell in love with Taos.

Top: strumming the day away

Phillips moved in right away. Blumenschein visited every summer until 1919, when he, his wife Mary Greene Blumenschein (also an artist), and daughter Helen bought this old adobe and moved here permanently. Their home is furnished minimally, with simple beds, tables, and chairs, and day beds that do double duty as couches and guest beds. Artwork abounds, however, with paintings by 'Blumy' and his contemporaries on every wall.

In 1912, Blumenschein and Phillips organized the Taos Society of Artists in the living room of Bert's sister Helen and her husband, Doc Martin. The Martin home is now incorporated into the 1936 **Historic Taos Inn** (125 Paseo del Norte, tel: 888/518-8267), the Taos equivalent of the landmark La Fonda in Santa Fe. Rooms here are atmospherically southwestern, with dark viga ceilings, plaster walls, and antiques. Some have *kiva* fireplaces. Dinner in **Doc Martin's Restaurant** is *the* place on Night One. The restaurant has a huge wine cellar and serves Nouvelle New Mexican cuisine that won't break the bank. If nothing else, drop into the **Adobe Bar** for a drink. There's live flamenco, jazz, and other music nightly. This is a great place to run into local people.

Paintings of churches, villages, mountains, Taos Pueblo elders, cowboys, and other frontier characters by Blumenstein, Phillips, Sharp, Victor Higgins, John Marin, Marsden Hartley, Dorothy Brett, and other Taos Society artists can be found in several museums in downtown Taos. **Harwood Museum of Art** (238 Ledoux St, tel: 505/758-9826; Tues–Sat 10am–5pm; admission) is the second-oldest museum in the state.

It was founded in the family adobe in 1923 by the widow of artist Burt Harwood who came to Taos for his health in the early 1900s. In 1936, the University of New Mexico began administering the museum and hired Santa Fe-Style architect John Gaw Meem to create an elegant expansion.

For my money, the Harwood's exhibit of Taos Society art is the best in town. The museum also displays unusual *bultos,* or saint statues, carved by master *santero* Patricio Barela in the 1940s and rare articulated *bultos* donated by Mabel Dodge Luhan. Contemporary galleries display works by minimalist artist Agnes Martin and changing exhibits by 20th-century modernists like Jackson Pollock.

There's a similar juxtaposition of old and new at the **Fechin Institute** (227 Paseo del Pueblo Norte, tel: 505/758-1710; Wed–Sun 10am–2pm; admission), a Taos museum you should not miss. The present building was created between 1927 and 1933 by renowned immigrant Russian painter Nicholai Fechin from an historic adobe. The son of a woodcarver, Fechin carved all

Right: E.L. Blumenschein Home and Museum

the furniture, doors, windows, and corbels in the house, which seamlessly blends a Russian monastic interior with traditional northern New Mexico exterior. Fechin's daughter Eya left the home to the city of Taos when she died. It has now been renovated to house the **Van Vechten-Lineberry Collection**. Fechin's exuberantly colored portraits and detailed drawings share space with fine originals by Taos Moderns like Larry Bell and the Taos Society of Artists.

Mabel Dodge Luhan wasn't the only strong-willed woman to come to Taos. In 1947, beautiful oil heiress Millicent Rogers gave Taos's most

formidable hostess a run for her money when she moved to town and, in the five short years before her tragic death at age 50, accumulated one of the premier collections of southwestern art in the region. After she died, her collection was put on public display in a private home a few miles northwest of Downtown. The **Millicent Rogers Museum** (Millicent Rogers Rd, tel: 505/758-2462; daily 10am–5pm, closed Mon Nov–Mar; admission) is an excellent place to get an overview of the historic and contemporary art of the Southwest.

Room after room holds dazzling collections of Navajo rugs, Hopi kachinas, painted and carved Hispanic *santos* and furniture, old and new Pueblo pottery, and Apache baskets. The collection of pottery by famed San Ildefonso potter María Martínez and her family alone warrants a visit to this museum. It is the only such collection donated by the potter's family and provides numerous intimate details about the creative interplay between generations, including letters, drawings, and family snapshots.

When Rogers moved to Taos, she adapted the traditional velvet dress of Navajo women into a unique personal statement and amassed an extraordinary collection of silver, turquoise, coral, and inlaid shell Indian jewelry. Many of her own designs are displayed here, along with her mother's important collection of paintings by Indian women artists like Pop Chalee, taught by Dorothy Dunn in The Studio in Santa Fe in 1932.

Since this museum is just outside town, I suggest visiting it on Day Two of this tour, when you can combine it with attractions along US 64, the main northbound highway out of Taos. Stay on US 64, after its junction with NM 522 and 150, and you'll soon come to the 650-ft-(200-m-) high **Rio Grande Gorge Bridge**, the second-highest suspension bridge in the nation. This span was dubbed the 'Bridge to Nowhere' when it was built in 1965, because the road then dead-ended on the other side of the gorge.

Turn right on NM 150 for the scenic road to **Taos Ski Valley**. This ski area is known worldwide for its excellent ski conditions and the annual

Top: folk art painting from the Millicent Rogers Museum, Taos

winter Taos Mountain Film Festival, a celluloid celebration of international mountain living. There are good restaurants just before you get to the charming village of **Arroyo Seco**, worth a stop for its galleries. **Momentitos de la Vida**, one of Taos's best dinner restaurants, has all the ambiance of a country inn, surrounded by pastures, grazing horses, and looming **Taos Mountain**, which turns bright pink at sunset.

Taos's biggest attraction by far is **Taos Pueblo** (tel: 505/758-1028), 3 miles (5km) northeast of town, off Pueblo de Taos Road. The main pueblo – an architectural icon – is thought to have been built between AD1000 and 1450, making it one of the oldest continuously occupied communities in the USA. It incorporates 99,000 acres (40,000 hectares), including land along the Rio Grande and 48,000-acre (19,500-hectare) Blue Lake on Taos Mountain, which was taken from the tribe in 1906 to become part of the national forest and returned in 1970, following a long fight with the federal government.

Today, Taos Pueblo is recognized as both a UNESCO World Heritage Site and a National Historic Landmark. But you'll find no 'museum Indians' here. This is a modern pueblo whose members wear contemporary attire, except on ceremonial days. Most work in nearby Taos or run tribal enterprises, such as galleries, horseback riding tours, and the tribe's small Mountain Casino.

About 150 tribal members live in the old pueblo, where, by tribal decree, no electricity or plumbing is allowed and all drinking water comes from the Rio del Pueblo. Because of the restrictions, most of the 1,800 other tribal members live

Top: Taos Pueblo, a World Heritage site
Right: shopping is excellent in Taos

nearby but maintain family buildings in Old Taos Pueblo for ceremonial purposes, and as art galleries, where you can buy micaceous pottery, beadwork, moccasins, and Taos's famous drums, which can be heard all over town.

The pueblo is open 7 days a week, from 8am to 4:30pm, except for 10 weeks in spring, when it closes for ceremonial purposes. Separate fees are charged for admission, photography, videotaping, and sketching. Pay the money. This is one experience you'll want to remember. Traditional dances take place year round. Taos Pueblo's Christmas Eve Mass of the Virgin in the

1850 **Church of San Gerónimo**, on the South Plaza, is New Mexico's most famous Christmas celebration. Thousands flock to the pueblo each year for the 400-year-old ritual which combines Catholic beliefs with the mysteries of Pueblo ceremonial life.

The Enchanted Circle

The 86-mile (138km) scenic byway known as the Enchanted Circle begins north of the Ski Valley turnoff and loops east at the artsy town of **Questa**, around 13,161-ft (4,012-m) **Wheeler Peak**, New Mexico's tallest mountain, via NM 38.

The loop passes through several former mining towns, including 1892 **Red River** – now a somewhat garish, family-oriented ski resort adjoining Bobcat Pass – and the more pleasant **Elizabethtown** in the Moreno Valley, where a small museum recalls the mining ghost town's rowdier days. Views of Wheeler Peak are spectacular at **Eagle Nest Lake**, a popular fishing spot now owned by the state, and **Angel Fire** ski resort, one of New Mexico's fastest-growing communities. At the junction of NM 38 and US 64, you can either continue east through scenic Cimarron Canyon and pick up the Old Santa Fe Trail, or head back to Taos via **Taos Canyon**, which has many art galleries along a steep, winding road.

Two stops on this tour stand out. Just beyond Arroyo Hondo, a right turn at San Cristobal takes you on a dirt road to Lobo Mountain, where the University of New Mexico preserves the **D.H. Lawrence Ranch**. The 160-acre (65-hectare) Kiowa Ranch was given to the writer and his wife Frieda by Mabel Dodge Luhan in 1924, when Lawrence returned to New Mexico aiming to create a Utopian community he called Rananim. During the summers of 1924 and 1925, the Lawrences and their only convert, Lady Dorothy Brett, together with Taos Pueblo artist Trinidad Archuleta and his wife, experimented with group living, painting, writing, fixing up cabins, milking cows, plowing fields, and baking bread.

The 14-month experiment ended when Lawrence was diagnosed with tuberculosis and he return to Europe. Before he died in Vence, France, in

Top: D.H. Lawrence Ranch
Right: Vietnam Veterans National Memorial

1930, Lawrence wrote about his New Mexico experiences in several novels and essays. 'There is something savage and unbreakable in the spirit of the place out here,' he wrote. 'It is good to be alone and responsible. But it is also very hard living up against these savage Rockies.'

In 1935, Frieda's lover Angelo Ravagli brought the writer's ashes back, and he was interred in a small whitewashed concrete shrine at the ranch. At her request, Frieda is buried outside the **Lawrence Memorial**, where a break in the forest offers spectacular views. Frieda Lawrence willed the ranch to the University of New Mexico, and the public is welcome to visit.

For fans of D.H. Lawrence, a pilgrimage to this shrine is one of the highlights of a visit to northern New Mexico. Be sure to allow enough time to soak up the atmosphere at this special place, where the wind moans gently through the pine trees and the silence and clear mountain air are inspiring. Ask the caretaker to show you the Lawrences' former cabin and a painting on a building wall by Trinidad Archuleta. Nearby is a bench beneath a huge, gnarled ponderosa pine, which became the subject of one of Georgia O'Keeffe's most famous paintings: the 1929 *Lawrence Tree*.

Equally inspiring, but for different reasons, is the **Vietnam Veterans National Memorial** (tel: 505/877-613-6900), high on a hillside near the turnoff for Angel Fire. Funded by Dr Victor Westphall in 1971 to honor the memory of his son David, who was killed with 12 comrades in Vietnam in 1968, this is a place where, like the phoenix above Lawrence's shrine, you feel the spirit reborn and flying free. A slender whitewashed building designed in the shape of a pair of folded dove's wings encloses an intimate chapel containing a small altar and photographs of the deceased. It's a moving experience to sit on one of the meditation cushions and listen to the wind moaning in the eaves.

The site is now recognized as a national memorial and has a well-conceived visitor center. An attractive museum uses artifacts, blow-up photographs, and quotations to get across its message of the futility of war. A powerful PBS documentary, drawing on home-movie footage, soldiers' letters home, and contemporary music, captures the reality of the Vietnamese experience.

3. O'KEEFFE COUNTRY *(see map, p48)*

This tour of the landscapes and Hispanic farming villages of the Chama River valley painted by Georgia O'Keeffe is essential for any fan of the US's most famous 20th-century female artist. It can be done from Santa Fe as one long day trip. If you're riding the Cumbres and Toltec Narrow Gauge Railroad (10am Tues and Sat; tel: **888/286-2737**), which takes you into the San Juan Mountains between Chama, New Mexico, and Antonito, Colorado, add another day. The train is popular, particularly during fall color rides in September, so reserve ahead of time.

A tour of the country Georgia O'Keeffe called home begins in **Española**,

a busy agricultural center 20 minutes north of Santa Fe, at the junction of US 84 and 285. Founded in the 1800s, Española today is an odd mix of traditional and contemporary. Here the drive-through Saints and Sinner's Liquor Store sits across the road from the **Oasis Cyber Café** (a good place for your morning caffeine fix).

Española has always been at the crossroads of history. Two miles (3km) north of town, adjoining the Towa village of San Juan Pueblo, are the ruins of New Mexico's first capital, founded by Don Juan de Oñate in 1598. Another former Spanish colonial settlement, **Santa Cruz**, is 3 miles (5km) east of Española. Founded by Don Diego de Vargas in 1693, it was for some years second in size only to Santa Fe.

The people of **San Juan Pueblo** (tel: 505/852-4400), who in the 1500s were living in two vil-

Top: Ghost Ranch landscape
Left: Georgia O'Keeffe, *circa* 1940

lages – Ok'he and Yunge – were the first to bear the brunt of Spanish colonization. When Oñate and his 400 settlers arrived in New Mexico, they first moved into Ok'he, which Oñate renamed San Juan de los Caballeros. When this site proved inhospitable, he took over Yunge and renamed it San Gabriel. In 1675, a San Juan religious leader named Popé was flogged for practicing what the padres regarded as sorcery. Soon after, Popé plotted an uprising that resulted in the Pueblo Revolt of 1680.

Today, San Juan Pueblo – one of the largest New Mexican pueblos – serves as the administrative headquarters of the Eight Northern Indian Pueblos, home to the attractive **Eight Northern Indian Pueblos Visitors Center** (tel: 505/852-4265). As well as offering an information center, museum, and gift shop, the building hosts the annual Eight Northern Indian Pueblos Artists and Craftsmen Show. The other highlight of the year is the pueblo's feast day on June 24, when hundreds of traditional dancers throng the plaza. The O'Ke Oweegne Arts and Crafts Cooperative is a good place to buy the pueblo's famous incised red pottery.

The modern residents of San Juan Pueblo are descendants of immigrants from the Mesa Verde area of Colorado, who moved south to the Rio Grande following a long drought in the 1200s. They built farming villages on river terraces throughout the Chama valley, spacing them roughly a day's walk, or 5 miles (8km) apart. The remains of the 700-room pueblo of **Poshouingue** can be seen from a half-mile trail off US 84, just south of Abiquíu. Poshouingue was inhabited for about a century before its residents moved on.

A few Spanish families founded the village of **Santa Rosa de Lima**, 3 miles (5km) south of modern-day Abiquíu, in 1734. They were forced to abandon it after several colonists were killed by Comanches. You can still see the cross and ruined adobe church on the right-hand side of the road, next to the Chama River. In 1754, a group of *genizaros* – former Indian captives who had become Hispanicized – moved 3 miles (5km) upriver to settle a former Indian pueblo, which they named Santo Tomás de Abiquíu.

Santa Rosa is long gone but **Abiquíu** was an instant success. Its open-door policy was a magnet for settlers unable to get ahead in socially conscious Santa Fe. By 1793, Abiquíu had a population of 1,363 and was New Mexico's third-largest town.

Its location on a cultural frontier was an advantage. Plains Indians arrived every fall to trade deerskins for Spanish horses, corn, and slaves. By the mid-1800s, trade at Abiquíu equaled that of Taos. One store was owned by Taos entrepreneur and former mountain man Ceran St Vrain. The army also used

Right: crosses at a meeting house of the secretive Penitente fraternity, near Abiquíu

the village as a base from which to patrol the surrounding area for Navajos, Jicarilla Apaches, and Utes. From 1852 to 1873, Abiquíu was headquarters for a Ute Indian Agency and trading post. It was the birthplace of Ouray, the leader of the Western Utes, who rose to fame during Colorado's Ute Indian Wars in the 1870s.

I mention Abiquíu's history at such length because although Abiquíu is famous, you won't find any museums or interpretive plaques in this sleepy village on the hill. In fact, there's little left to remind anyone of Abiquíu's former importance, except crumbling adobes and a lovely 1940s church designed by John Gaw Meem. Abiquíu's fame today principally resides in its location as the home of Georgia O'Keeffe, who bought a sprawling, ruined adobe *hacienda* near the entrance to the village in 1945 and moved

here in 1949, after a four-year remodeling of the 3-acre (1.2-hectare) property. From then on, O'Keeffe spent winters in Abiquíu and summers at her Ghost Ranch property until ill health forced her to move to Santa Fe in 1984. She died there in 1986 at the age of 98.

The **Georgia O'Keeffe Home** is a walled oasis, with shade trees, flower beds, and a vegetable garden watered by the community *acequia*. Inside, thrifty and ingenious midwestern touches, such as cupboards built into thick adobe walls and well-maintained mangles, refrigerators, and other 1950s appliances, blend seamlessly with floor-to-ceiling windows and elegant Eames chairs brought from her home in New York.

The Georgia O'Keeffe Foundation, headed up by O'Keeffe's last companion, New Mexico photographer and ceramicist Juan Hamilton, runs one-hour tours of the house by appointment only on Tuesday, Thursday, and Friday, April to November. Group size is limited to 12 people; call well in advance for reservations (tel: 505/685-4539).

Tours of the O'Keeffe property begin at the foundation's offices, across the street in the **Abiquíu Inn** (tel: 505/685-4328). The attractive adobe complex has several nice *casitas* that are a pleasant and inexpensive place to spend the night. A restaurant serves Middle Eastern and New Mexico meals. The inn is part of the 1,600 acres (650 hectares) owned by **Dar Al Islam** (tel: 505/685-4515), which began building a Muslim community here in the 1980s that has since been reorganized into an educational and retreat center. Its large mosque, designed by renowned Egyptian architect Hassan Fathi, is behind the inn, off FR 155, close to Georgia O'Keeffe's favored walking area: the White Place. Visitors are welcome.

Dar Al Islam isn't the only religious community that has made its home here. **Monastery of Christ in the Desert** (www.christdesert.org) was built by Benedictine monks in 1962 and is located 13 miles (21km) down FR 151

Above: scene along US 84 near Georgia O'Keeffe's Abiquíu home

in Chama River Canyon, 27 miles (44km) north of Abiquíu. You are welcome to visit and hike, meditate, and enjoy the silence. For longer personal retreats, you can arrange to stay in the monastery's guest-house. Contact the monastery online or drop in to their gift shop, which sells *retablos,* tinwork, incense, and other crafts. Christmas services in the church are worth making a special trip.

Ghost Ranch Conference Center (tel: 877/804-4678), 12 miles (19km) northwest of Abiquíu, offers a retreat center of a dif-ferent sort. This former dude ranch, now owned by the Presbyterian Church, has a wealth of activities on its extensive prop-erty. Day visitors are welcome to hike into the colorful canyons behind the center, where paleontologists have uncovered rare dinosaurs, and visit the **Florence Hawley Ellis Anthropology Museum** and the **Ruth Hall Paleontology Museum**, both of which have information on the area's geology and natural history. Longer residential workshops are held here regularly, where inexpensive lodging and meals are available. Ghost Ranch is also the last developed campground on US 84 north before you get into the San Juan Mountains, and is worth stopping to see.

From **Ghost Ranch**, you have a good view of **Pedernal**, one of Georgia O'Keeffe's favorite subjects. She once said that God told her if she painted it often enough, He'd give it to her. In a way He did. She's buried on the moun-tain. All around Pedernal is the colorful, eroded canyon country of the mile-high Colorado Plateau, best known for spectacular geological parks like Arizona's Grand Canyon. Erosion also created **Echo Amphitheater,** about

3 miles (5km) north of Ghost Ranch, an enormous amphitheater in the sandstone cliffs. It makes a nice stop to stretch your legs or have a picnic (plan ahead by buying food at the classic 1940s **Bode's Mercantile**, in Abiquíu, before you leave.)

The craggy profile of the San Juan Mountains walls the northern sky-line as you head north on US 84 into the Tierra Amarilla valley. You're really in high country now, where snowmelt from the mountains trick-les through lush pastures laced with delicate, pastel spring wildflowers. The courageous people who founded

Top: Ghost Ranch rocks
Right: Ghost Ranch ruins

Tierra Amarilla, Los Brazos, and Los Ojos in 1860 were sheepherders and farmers from Abiquíu. Emboldened by the presence of US soldiers, they built communities on the common lands, or *ejidos*, of the 1832 Mexican land grant they had been grazing for decades. A hundred years later, the loss of those lands, following a US court decision revoking their communal status, ignited a firestorm over the inequities of land distribution in northern New Mexico. In 1967, a group of armed Hispanic men led by the charismatic Reies López Tijerina stormed the courthouse in Tierra Amarilla, aiming to make a citizen's arrest of the district attorney. Angered by the D.A.'s absence, the men shot up the courthouse, wounded two lawmen, and fled with two hostages before being captured by the National Guard.

Although the resistance failed, the publicity jumpstarted a number of social programs aimed at helping these communities become self-sustaining. In the 1990s, the nonprofit Ganados del Valle began a women's weaving cooperative using the long-fibered wool of locally reared churro sheep, the hardy breed brought to New Mexico by Spanish settlers 400 years earlier.

A visit to **Tierra Wools** (91 Main St, Los Ojos, tel: 505/588-7231) offers a glimpse into the soul of Hispanic culture in northern New Mexico. Here you can watch freshly sheared wool being graded, hand spun, and colored with natural dyes, and purchase beautiful blankets and jackets woven on looms in the back. These are highly coveted items. Other Ganados del Valle businesses are showcased in **Los Pastores** (tel: 505/588-0020), an 1890 general store next door.

If you're riding the **Cumbres and Toltec Scenic Railroad**, stay at one of the bed and breakfasts in the Tierra Amarilla valley or in Chama

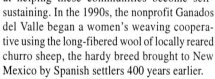

Top: desert views made famous by Georgia O'Keeffe
Left: Cumbres and Toltec Scenic Railroad

excursions

itself, opposite the historic rail depot. The railroad was built in 1880 to serve mining camps in the San Juan Mountains and revived in the 1960s. The 64-mile (103-km), one-way train trip leaves Chama twice a week in summer and fall; bus transportation is available for the return journey. Chama is surrounded by **Carson National Forest**, a good place for camping and hiking. There are numerous pullouts, campgrounds, and picnic spots on scenic NM 64, which takes you east into the Tusas Mountains, south of Chama, to **Tres Piedras**, where you can either continue to Taos via the Rio Grande Gorge or loop back to Española via US 285.

After a long day sitting in trains and cars, there's nothing better than a soak at **Ojo Caliente Hot Springs and Spa** (50 Los Baños Drive, Ojo Caliente, tel: 505/583-2233), which has been in use for more than a thousand years. Dip in and out of different pools containing unique combinations of mineralized hot springs. New owners are presently upgrading the aging property. Offerings include a mud pool, private cliffside tubs, massage and bodywork services in the bathhouse, spa cuisine, and several new cabins in addition to basic rooms in the historic 1916 hotel.

If you really want to push the boat out, you'll book a room at nearby **Rancho de San Juan** (US 285, Ojo Caliente, tel: 505/753-6818). You wouldn't expect to find one of the West's most luxurious B&Bs in these arid foothills, but here it is. Rancho de San Juan has been a hit ever since it opened and consistently tops critic's lists, not only for its elegant rooms and *casitas* but its award-winning, four-course, fixed-price dinners. Dinner is open to non-guests, but book ahead.

4. SANTA FE TRAIL *(map, p48)*

This overnight trip through the valleys and grasslands of northeastern New Mexico follows the former route of the Santa Fe Trail. The landmarks remain the same: the Sangre de Cristo Mountains, the easternmost young volcano field in the country, an ancient Indian pueblo, a former US Army fort, Old West towns, hot springs, and wildlife preserves filled with migratory birds, bison, and pronghorn antelope.

Start this excursion by driving south out of Santa Fe on Old Pecos Trail. Turn left just before Interstate 25 onto Old Las Vegas Highway and stop about a half-mile down on the left for breakfast at **Harry's Roadhouse** *(see page 29)*. This popular local haven is always busy, so get here early to avoid the brunch crowd. After breakfast, return to Interstate 25 and drive east through scenic Glorieta Pass to the tiny Hispanic village

Right: dressed up and ready to hit the trail

of **Pecos**, about 40 minutes from Santa Fe. As you enter the Pecos River valley, the 13,000-ft (4,000-m) Sangre de Cristo Mountains are to the north and the Tecolote Mountains and their western extension, Glorieta Mesa, are to the south. Exit the freeway at the Rowe exit and follow signs on NM 63 for **Pecos National Historical Park** (tel: 505/757-6032; daily 8am–5pm, until 6pm in summer; admission).

After 1858, one of the last rest stops before reaching Santa Fe was **Kozlowski's Stage Stop**, 3 miles (5km) east of Pecos, where travelers enjoyed Mrs Kozlowski's famous fried trout, pulled from the icy waters of the Pecos River, and visited the nearby ruins of Pecos Pueblo.

By the time Kozlowski built his stage stop, using timbers from the ruined Spanish mission church at Pecos, the powerful 15th-century trading pueblo of Cicuye – a magnificent, 650-room, fortified city-state dominating the frontier between the Rio Grande pueblos and the Plains – had been empty for about 20 years. Its former residents had migrated to live with Towa-speaking relatives at Jémez Pueblo, on the other side of the Rio Grande. In its heyday, though, the multi-story pueblo inspired awe in all who saw it. Even the Spaniards, whose zealous missionary efforts and foreign diseases doomed the population, were impressed.

Pay your fee in the E.E. Fogelson Visitor Center (named for the husband of actress Greer Garson, who donated the land to the park service for the park). Be sure to visit the museum, which displays more than 80,000 artifacts excavated from Pecos by A.V. Kidder, the father of Southwest archeology.

The remains of the old pueblo and mission church are a little over a mile behind the visitor center, along a paved trail. The park offers tours of nearby Civil War sites, Santa Fe Trail ruts (next to the visitor center), and the **Forked Lightning Ranch House**, designed for rodeo entrepreneur Tex Austin in 1926 by John Gaw Meem. There are also daily demonstrations of breadmaking, basketry, blacksmithing, and silversmithing at Kozlowski's Trading Post (now part of the park) during the summer months.

Take a break at **Frankie's** (tel:

Top: painted church in a desert sky
Right: Las Vegas hospitality since 1882

505/757-3322), just north of the park, for some delicious New Mexico pinyon-flavored coffee and a slice of homemade cake (if it's lunchtime, try the bottomless green chile stew or a fresh-off-the-grill breakfast burrito). Then return to Interstate 25 and continue another 20 minutes east to **Las Vegas** (named for its location at the edge of the Plains). A lot of visitors miss Las Vegas, or confuse it with the glittering, neon city in Nevada. That's a pity because this wonderful old Victorian town has a lot to offer: several institutions of higher learning, bird-watching at Las Vegas National Wildlife Refuge, and one of the state's most extensive historic districts.

Take the downtown walking tour to see some of the 900 listed structures, from nicely restored Victorian brick buildings like the 1882 **Plaza Hotel** (230 Plaza, tel: 800/328-1882), to leaning Spanish colonial adobe homes on winding side streets. At the turn of the 20th century, Teddy Roosevelt blew into town and recruited scores of Spanish-speaking volunteers for his team of 'Rough Riders.' Find out more about New Mexico's prominent role in the Spanish-American War at the **Rough Riders Museum** (725 Grand Ave, tel: 505/454-1401, ext 283; Mon–Fri 9am–noon, 1–4pm), a quirky little institution typical of small-town America.

Haye Springs Well, situated at 2213 Hot Springs Boulevard, is the oldest surviving well on the Santa Fe Trail. Las Vegas boomed when the railroad reached the town, and by 1900 it had a greater population than Santa Fe. Every summer, adventurous wealthy folk rode the rails west to enjoy luxury resorts built by entrepreneurs like Fred Harvey. One of the most exclusive lies 5 miles/8km northwest of town, off NM 65, at the mouth of Gallinas Canyon. **Montezuma Castle** (tel: 505/454-4200) was an elegant Grande Dame hotel built around mountain hot springs. A multimillion-dollar restoration by United World College, a small private school attracting students from around the world, has returned the building to its former glory. The hot springs are open to the public for free.

If you're short on time, dine in Las Vegas and return to Santa Fe, an hour away. Alternatively, check into the Plaza, then continue exploring the next day. Nineteen miles east of Las Vegas is **Fort Union National Monument**

Top: handsome Victorian buildings, Las Vegas, New Mexico

(NM 161, 8 miles/13km northwest of Interstate 25, tel: 505/425-8025; daily 8am–6pm; admission), which was once one of the largest and most important forts in the West. Built in 1851, close to where the Mountain and Cimarron Cutoff branches of the Santa Fe Trail converged (trail ruts are very easy to see), the fort served as a supply depot for other military outposts in the Southwest. Its most important role, however, was to protect travelers. Two replacements were later built, but by 1891 the fort was abandoned. You'll find exhibits on the Santa Fe Trail in the museum.

If you're traveling during the summer, you might also want to visit the **Santa Fe Trail Museum** (614 Maxwell Ave; 9am–4pm; admission) in **Springer**, about a half-hour on, at the US 56 exit from the freeway. US 56 continues south near the **Mills Canyon** unit of **Kiowa National Grassland** (714 Main St, Clayton, tel: 505/374-9652), a good place to spot pronghorn, the fastest animal on the continent. If you stay on US 56, you'll reach **Clayton**, where you can visit the McNee's Crossing section of the Santa Fe Trail, just east of town.

Just north of Springer, pick up NM 21 and drive through the last intact section of the historic 1.7 million-acre (690,000-hectare) **Maxwell Land Grant**, amassed in 1847 by former mountain man Lucien Maxwell. The largest ranches in the area can be found on remaining segments of the old land grant, including **Vermejo Park Ranch**, a luxury hunting resort owned by media mogul Ted Turner.

A large section of the land grant, south of Cimarron, was bought in 1922 by Waite Phillips, founder of Phillips Oil. Phillips donated the large property to the Boy Scouts of America in 1938. **Philmont Boy Scout Ranch** (tel: 505/376-2281) is now used by thousands of scouts to test their backcountry skills. You can tour Waite's Mediterranean-style **Villa Philmonte** and

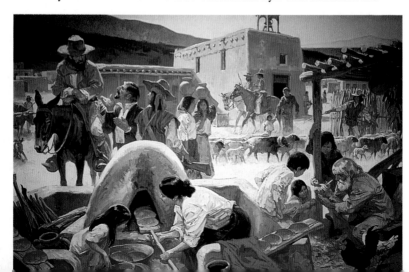

enjoy living-history demonstrations at the **Kit Carson Home and Museum** in Rayado. The **Philmont Museum** and **Seton Library** are open year round. Bison and other wildlife are visible from the highway in winter. You can also see bison on the **Maxwell National Wildlife Refuge** (tel: 505/375-2331), near Maxwell, as well as some 200 species of birds, including burrowing owls and overwintering geese and ducks attracted to the irrigation lakes of this expansive ranch country.

Maxwell planned to capitalize on traffic on the Santa Fe Trail. In 1864, he built the **Aztec Grist Mill** (tel: 505/376-2913) in Cimarron and supplied flour to the US Army and Jicarilla Indian Agency. The four-story Aztec Mill is now a museum run by the CS Cattle Company. It's open only on summer weekends. The mill is just one of 14 historic locations on a fascinating downtown walking tour of **Cimarron**, named by early Spaniards whose run-ins with local Apaches and Utes led them to call the area *cimarron,* wild and unruly.

The undisputed highlight is the 1880 **St James Hotel** (tel: 800/748-2694). The St James was built by Henri Lambert, former cook for Abraham Lincoln, and was the first hotel west of the Mississippi to offer running water, gourmet food, and luxurious furnishings. Buffalo Bill planned his Wild West shows in the bar with Annie Oakley, and notorious figures like Bat Masterson, Blackjack Ketchum, and Jesse James were frequent guests.

The hotel's 1872 saloon (now a dining room serving highly rated steaks and other fare) was famously violent, as numerous bullet holes in the pressed-tin ceiling attest. The hotel's new owner, Roger Smith, mayor of neighboring Colfax, has ensured that guests have an authentic Wild West experience. That includes ghosts. If you stay in Lambert's wife's former room, you'll likely smell roses. The room of one decidedly restless ghost is off limits. The specter, a man named TJ, allegedly won the hotel in a poker game but was gunned down before collecting his prize.

Finish this tour by driving south on US 64 to **Capulin Volcano National Monument** (off NM 325, just north of Capulin, tel: 505/278-2201; daily 7:30am–6:30pm in summer, 8am–4pm in winter; admission), a wonderful spot for taking in the lay of the land. Capulin, a pleasingly symmetrical cinder cone rising 1,400ft (425m) above the surrounding grasslands, was born about 60,000 years ago, a comparative youngster in the 8,000-sq-mile (21,000-sq-km) Raton-Clayton Volcanic Field. Don't bypass this little national monument; it's a true gem.

A historic 2-mile (3-km) road winds up to the 8,182-ft (2,494-m) summit. From here you can hike the short **Crater Vent Trail** or circle the rim on a mile-long trail that offers unparalled views of nearby volcanoes and the states of Texas, Oklahoma, Colorado, and Kansas.

Top left: you're never alone on a ranch. **Left:** scene depicting the old Southwest **Right:** Capulin Volcano rises above grasslands scattered with volcanic rock

5. THE SCENIC TURQUOISE TRAIL TO ALBUQUERQUE
(see maps, p48 and p74)

This backroad journey through the mountains southeast of Santa Fe leads to Albuquerque, via mining ghost towns resurrected by artists, quirky home-grown museums, and forested trails on the Sandia Crest. Spend the night in Albuquerque and explore Route 66, from Old Town to Nob Hill, where you can soak up atmosphere, excellent museums, and good food before heading to the airport.

Have breakfast in Santa Fe, then drive south on Interstate 25 to the NM 14 turnoff and head toward Madrid (pronounced MAD-rid) on the scenic byway

the **Turquoise Trail** (www.turquoise-trail.com). The road winds through an area of hills, arroyos, and dramatically upended rocks known as the **Garden of the Gods**, the northwestern margin of the **Galisteo Basin**. The **Cerrillos Historic Mining District** is the oldest in the US. By AD1000, turquoise mining camps were supplying the precious stones for trade to the Aztec Empire in Mexico.

In 1541, Coronado and his Spanish *conquistadores* passed through the Galisteo Basin. They missed the mines, but by the early 1600s, New Mexico's first administrator, Juan de Oñate, was mining silver and lead at Cerrillos, which may predate Santa Fe as the first colonial settlement in this area.

In 1879, American miners from Leadville, Colorado, flooded into the area. They laid out the village of **Cerrillos** in 1880, the year the railroad reached the area. Cerrillos is pretty sleepy now, but in its heyday it boasted 3,000 residents, 21 saloons, five brothels, four hotels, and eight newspapers. The **Clear Light Opera House**, where Sarah Bernhardt and Lily Langtry sang, is still on Main Street, and over a dozen movies have been shot here. Residents succeeded in getting 1,100 acres (445 hectares) of the former mining district set aside as open space. **Cerrillos Hills Historic Park** (tel: 505/995-2074) has hiking trails and informative signs and is worth a stop.

Nearby **Madrid** is the oldest coal-mining region in New Mexico, with mines dating to the mid-1850s. The town really took off in 1892, when a railroad spur linked the mining town, then known as Coal Gulch, to the main line of the Santa Fe Railroad at Lamy. By the early 1900s, Madrid was owned by the Albuquerque and Cerrillos Coal Company and had a population of 2,500. The company built schools, a hospital, a company store, a tavern, and an employees club. Miners were required to donate to civic causes and participate in town events, such as Madrid's famous Christmas illuminations,

Top: Sandia Crest tramway

excursions

which consisted of 150,000 Christmas lights powered by 500,000 kilowatts of electricity from the town's coal-fed generators. Madrid's ballpark was the first floodlit stadium in the country.

In the mid-1970s, the town's then owner, the son of the former mine superintendent, sold aging miner's homes to artists and other counter-culture types unable to afford Santa Fe prices. Today, 300 residents run a plethora of art galleries, cafés, restaurants, museums, and bed-and-breakfasts. The **Madrid Holiday Open House** (tel: 505/471-1054), featuring those famous Christmas lights, is once again a popular tradition, and on summer weekends, bluegrass and jazz enthusiasts flock to the old stadium to listen to concerts.

Stop for lunch at the **Mine Shaft Tavern** (tel: 505/473-0743), which has the longest bar in New Mexico. On weekends, you'll meet all kinds of folks enjoying strong drinks, good burgers, and live music. The mine shaft itself can be viewed at the **Old Coal Mine Museum** (tel: 505/438-3780), which has exhibits on the town's history and a restored 1900 locomotive. Victorian melodramas are performed in the **Engine House Theater**.

About 12 miles (19km) south of **Golden**, site of the West's first gold rush in 1825, take a right on **Sandia Crest Scenic Byway** (NM 536), which winds to the top of 10,000-ft (3,000-m) Sandia Crest. This is a good place to hike in the summer months or ski in the winter months.

Two miles (3km) up the road, behind a wall made of thousands of glass bottles, you'll find quirky, fascinating **Tinkertown** (tel: 505/281-5333; Apr–Oct 9am–6pm; admission). A 30-year work-in-progress by wood carver Ross Ward and his potter wife Carla, this funky little museum displays a three-ring circus and a miniature Wild West town. There's nothing quite like it.

NM 14 passes through Cedar Crest then

Top: the longest bar in New Mexico
Right: quirky Tinkertown museum

joins Interstate 40 at Tijeras. Drive west on I-40 and take the Rio Grande Boulevard exit south towards New Mexico's biggest city, **Albuquerque**. Head first for the area called **Old Town**. This is where acting governor Francisco Cuervo y Valdez founded Albuquerque in 1706 on the site of a 1632 *estancia,* or ranch. The lively historic **Plaza** has a lot in common with Santa Fe's Plaza, but it's more Mexican in ambiance.

In June, a popular Old Town Fiesta brings mariachi music, food, dance, and celebrations to Old Town. Christmas Eve is even more atmospheric: the Plaza is bathed in the candlelight of thousands of brown bag *farolito* lanterns, lighting the way for the Christ Child. **San Felipe de Neri Church** was originally west of the Plaza but was moved to the north side in 1793. Although small, the church has a formal Catholic air to it, befitting a parish church where Mass is still held.

Albuquerque's must-see museums are all nearby. A block east of the church is the **Albuquerque Museum of Art and History** (2000 Mountain Rd NW, tel: 505/242-4600; Tues–Sun 9am–5pm; admission), which chronicles four centuries of Albuquerque history. Its *vaquero,* or Spanish cowboy, exhibit is particularly interesting, while the museum also has a wonderful collection of New Mexico

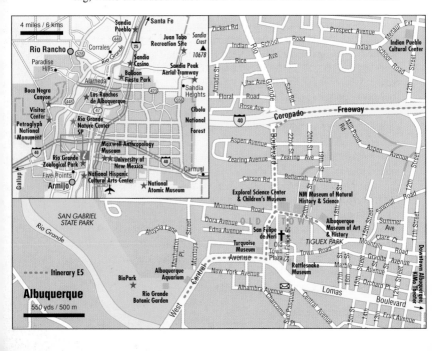

art, including works by Taos Society artists, Georgia O'Keeffe, Hispanic *enfant terrible* fiberglass artist Luis Jimenez, and Indian artists like sculptors Roxanne Swentzell and Allan Houser.

Explora! Science Center and Children's Museum (1803 Mountain Rd, tel: 505/842-1537; Mon–Sat 10am–6pm, Sun noon–6pm; admission) is a state-of-the-art museum with all the bells and whistles to keep kids absorbed, and more than 250 hands-on exhibits. On no account miss the **New Mexico Museum of Natural History and Science** (tel: 505/841-2800; daily 9am–6pm; admission) next door. This is *the* place to learn about New Mexico's numerous volcanoes, unusual dinosaurs, and importance as an astronomy center. The large-screen theater shows a variety of films, including one on chimp expert Jane Goodall.

If you have time, you can see real animals at **BioPark** (2601 W. Central Ave NW, tel: 505/764-6200; daily 9am–5pm; admission), which is really three separate facilities: an aquarium with exhibits of sharks, moray eels, and other Gulf of Mexico sea creatures; an adjoining botanical garden inter-

preting the Southwest's Chihuahuan and Sonoran deserts, which is both fun and educational; and, a few blocks away, a zoo, where the incongruous highlights are frisky polar bears keeping cool in an air-conditioned cave and a sparkling waterfall.

New Mexico has six remaining segments of old **Route 66** – the historic transcontinental road that brought thousands West between 1926 and the 1950s. Albuquerque's neon-lit **Central Avenue**, which goes cross-town from Old Town to the foothills of the Sandias, is one of the best preserved. **La Posada de Albuquerque** (125 Second St NW, tel: 505/242-9090), a block north of Central, was New Mexico native Conrad Hilton's first hotel in 1939 and is still one of Downtown's most charming buildings. Its Pueblo Revival lobby has a cool elegance, with dark mission-style wood furniture, an old-fashioned bar, ceiling *vigas*, and a fine wall mural of pueblos.

Spend the night at La Posada (it's surprisingly reasonable) and you can wander over to the section of Central known as **The District**. Downtown has the city's hippest clubs and restaurants, galleries, Western shops, and the beautiful **KiMo Theater**, one of the best examples of ornate Pueblo Deco architecture in the state.

Follow Central east under Interstate 25 to reach the **University of New Mexico** campus with its excellent **Maxwell Anthropology Museum** (tel: 505/277-4404; Tues–Fri 9am–4pm, Sat 10am–4pm; free), designed by John Gaw Meem. Nearby **Nob Hill** is a lively collegiate hotspot with some of the best-loved restaurants and shops in the Duke City.

Left: Albuquerque's neon-lit Central Avenue is part of old Route 66
Right: the KiMo Theater is one of New Mexico's best examples of Pueblo Deco

Leisure
Activities

SHOPPING

Santa Fe has many unique stores, from high-end art galleries and clothes boutiques to shops specializing in local products and bazaars selling imported items from Central America, Afghanistan, Tibet, and other exotic countries. In the historic Downtown, even franchise stores like Starbucks occupy renovated adobe buildings, and retail prices reflect stratospheric rents. Indoor shopping arcades adjoining hotels like La Fonda offer fabulous window displays, where you can drool over breathtaking Indian pottery, turquoise-and-silver jewelry, locally woven clothes, and other temptations.

Most locals avoid the congested downtown area and do their shopping in surrounding districts. Eastside residents favor the area opposite the New Mexico Capitol, on the corner of Old Santa Fe Trail and Paseo de Peralta, where you'll find **Kaune's Food Town**, one of the few family grocers still in business, and old-fashioned corner shops like **Four and Twenty Blackbirds**, dispensing fresh-baked pies on Fridays.

Guadalupe Historic District, two blocks west, has an eclectic mix of dance clubs, workout studios, open-air and indoor markets, specialty clothes shops, outdoor stores, restaurants, and natural foods emporiums adjoining the redeveloped Railyards. Santa Fe's newest up-and-coming scene is on the previously industrial **Second Street**, between Cerrillos and St Francis Drive, which has a mix of thrift stores, fitness studios, breweries, hairdressers, and cafés like **Cloud Cliff Bakery** and **Chocolate Maven**, *the* best bakers in town.

You'll find budget stores at the south end of **Cerrillos Road**, the busy, commercial corridor. **Villa Linda Mall** and its adjoining mall has a number of big-box stores, including Sears, Dillards, J.C. Penney, Mervyns, Walgreens, and Target. Walmart and K-Mart are nearby. **Santa Fe Premium Outlets** is about a mile south, at the NM 14/Interstate 24 exit, and has about 40 name-brand retailers offering good discounts, including Liz Claiborne, Jones New York, Peruvian Connection, and Sissel's Fine Indian Jewelry, Pottery, and Kachinas.

De Vargas Mall, about six blocks northwest of the Plaza, off Paseo de Peralta, has a nice blend of mainstream and specialty stores, including Starbucks, Albertsons supermarket, Ross discount clothes outlet, Las Cosas specialty cookware and foods, and other businesses. Both malls have busy movie complexes, post-office branches, and unique confections featuring chile and piñon nuts by local candy maker **Señor Murphy**. Hours are Mon–Sat 10am–9pm (noon–9pm Sun).

Santa Feans are free thinkers and love to read, and authors often visit independently owned bookstores. **Collected Works** on West San Francisco Street and **Garcia Books** on Garcia Street, off Canyon Road, have hosted Michael Moore, Sherman Alexie, Hillary Clinton, and other big names. **Downtown Subscription** café, which has the city's largest selection of international magazines and newspapers, is next to Garcia Books. **The Ark**, just west

Left: a sign of Santa Fe
Right: shop till you rock, New Mexico

pottery, while nearby **Morning Star Gallery** sells a wider selection of American Indian-made items, from Plains beadwork and *parfleche* to baskets from the Northwest and Southwestern kachinas, textiles, and pottery. **Dewey Galleries** (53 Old Santa Fe Trail) represents the late, highly regarded Chiricahua Apache sculptor Allan Houser and also has historic Indian weavings, pottery, jewelry, and artifacts.

Today's stars of the Santa Fe art world are often graduates of Santa Fe's well-respected Institute of American Indian Arts. Jicarilla Apache artist and musician Darren Vigil Gray's abstract paintings tackle mythic cultural themes and are collected by musicians of the caliber of Sir Paul McCartney and Robbie Robertson. He is represented by **Hahn Ross Gallery**.

Hispanic Folk Art

The tradition of making carved and painted religious items and furniture for use in churches and homes dates back to New Mexico's frontier days, when the long distance from Mexico City required self-sufficiency and creativity. Families living in villages along the High Road to Taos continue to specialize in certain crafts.

of the Railyards, is the place to head for spiritual books and New Age paraphernalia. **Travel Bug** on Paseo de Peralta carries the best selection of maps and guidebooks; slide shows and talks by writers take place most Saturdays at 5pm.

Native American Arts and Crafts

Santa Fe is a mecca for antique and contemporary American Indian art. **Packards Indian Trading Co** on the Plaza has been selling pottery by María Martínez, Nampeyo, and other Pueblo artists since 1920. On Canyon Road, **Michael Smith Gallery** focuses on antique Navajo rugs and Pueblo

These crafts include wood carving in Cordova; weaving in Chimayó; representations of the saints, or *santos*, such as *bultos* (statues), *retablos* (paintings), and *reredos* (carved and painted altar screens), in Truchas and Taos. New generations of Ortegas and Trujillos in Chimayó, Barelas in Taos, and

others still sell directly from home studios. The Museum of New Mexico stores or the Museum of Spanish Colonial Art are good places to find out who to collect and to buy authenticated pieces of art.

The Rainbow Man (107 E. Palace) has many fine examples of early Hispanic folk art as well as contemporary artists who sell their best work at July's annual **Spanish Market** on the Plaza. Elaborate *santos* by master carver Charlie Carrillo go for thousands of dollars but good work by youngsters can be had much cheaper.

You won't find the work of El Rito *santero* Nicholas Herrera at this traditional market. Herrera's car fender paintings, folksy tableaux, and icons pull no punches about the challenges of life in contemporary New Mexico villages and have become highly collectable. He is represented by **Cline Fine Art Gallery** on West Palace.

Art Galleries

Legend has it that Santa Fe is the third-largest art market in the US after New York and Los Angeles. True or not, artists of all kinds have been selling their work here for nearly a century. **Gerald Peters Gallery**, housed in a beautiful Santa Fe-style building on Paseo de Peralta, has works by Georgia O'Keeffe and early Taos and Santa Fe colony artists, such as Ernest Blumenschein and Fremont Ellis, as well as important historic Western artists such as Albert Bierstadt.

Sculptures by contemporary Santa Fe artists like nationally known Glenna Goodacre and others can be found next door at **Nedra Matteucci Gallery**. Several hundred other art galleries in the Santa Fe area specialize in everything from romantic southwestern landscapes to rough and ready cowboy art.

Santa Fe Style/Western & Vintage Clothes Stores

You'll find hundreds of styles of Wrangler's jeans, cowboy hats, cowboy boots, and tailored shirts with mother-of-pearl buttons at **Western Warehouse** in Villa Linda and De Vargas Malls. **Back at the Ranch** (209 East Marcy St) sells cowboy boots by Lucheesi and others and will make custom boots for you. Ever-popular **Doubletake** (320 Aztec

St) mixes 'pre-worn' and new items at its three budget stores in the Guadalupe district. There's a wonderful selection of vintage cowboy clothes at **Double Take at the Ranch** (317 S. Guadalupe, next to Cowgirl Bar-B-Q). **Lucille's** (223 Galisteo) specializes in Santa Fe Style, with lots of flowing skirts, dresses, and ruffles. **Judy's Unique Apparel** (724 Canyon Rd) is another longtime local favorite for distinctive men's and women's dress-up duds fashioned from velvet, silk, and other luxurious fabrics.

New Mexican Specialty Shops

Nambeware – beautiful, practical, and decorative items, from vases to dishes, made of a metal alloy containing no silver, lead, or pewter – make wonderful Santa Fe gifts. Nambe does not crack, chip, peel, or tarnish and the dishes can retain heat and cold for hours. You can find cheaper seconds at outlets on Paseo de Peralta and West San Francisco in Santa Fe; also look for Nambeware at outlets in Taos.

Jackalope (2820 Cerrillos) sells the city's largest and best-priced selection of local and imported items. Stock up on cheap Mexican rugs, terra-cotta pots, and religious icons made from found objects, and find gifts from Santa Fe or the Southwest for everyone you know. Look for locally made strings of red chile, pinyon-flavored coffee, anise-flavored *bizcochito* cookies, and jars of salsa, pinyon incense, and toiletries made from desert essences. They'll love you for it.

Top left: turquoise and silver are bargains. **Left:** a store in Madrid, New Mexico
Above: these boots are made for buying; you can even have them custom made

EATING OUT

In a state renowned for nurturing artists, cooking of every style is also considered an art form. Chefs like Coyote Café's Mark Miller and Café Pasqual's Katherine Kagel are inspired by the lively mix of Indian, Hispanic, and Anglo culinary traditions in New Mexico and have helped spark a renaissance in family farms by demanding organic produce and range-fed meat. Small growers now produce heirloom crops and specialty items, such as handmade goat's cheese and Indian-reared bison, along with chile – grown in vast quantities in Hatch and Chimayó – which infuses everything from beer to cheese, even fast-food hamburgers.

New Mexican food is centered on corn, squash, and beans. These important staples were introduced from Mexico more than 2,000 years ago and were quickly embraced by Pueblo people as an addition to wild foods such as plants and game. Spaniards later introduced potatoes, tomatoes, and chile peppers from Central and South America; avocados, grapes, and melons; spices like cinnamon and nutmeg from the Caribbean islands; and European fruit and wheat. But perhaps their most important innovation was ranching, a way of life now synonymous with the West.

No matter what your budget, you'll eat well in New Mexico. Daily standards include ranch-style eggs, or *huevos rancheros,* and filled wheat or corn tortillas, such as burritos and enchiladas smothered in piping hot chile sauce, made from fresh green or dried red chile (both together is a 'christmas'). A special meal might feature chile-marinated pork known as

carne adovada; green chile stew made with pork and *posole*, or hominy; steamed ground-corn *tamales* flavored with meat or cheese; and *flan*, the Spanish and Mexican version of crème caramel. Tiny anise-flavored cookies, or *bizcochitos*, are served with hot chocolate and cider at Christmas.

Price Guide
Based on the cost of a three-course meal for one, excluding drinks and tip:
$ = Inexpensive (under $15)
$$ = Moderate ($15–30)
$$$ = Expensive (over $30)

Note: other restaurants and cafés can be found in the relevant itinerary.

Santa Fe
Amaya at Hotel Santa Fe
1501 Paseo de Peralta, Santa Fe, NM 87501
Tel: 505/982-1200
Native American cuisine and New American specials combine in this fine restaurant. Try the mixed grill, featuring pan-seared bison tenderloin (from the herd owned by hotel majority owners Picurís Pueblo), mustard-rubbed lamb chop, elk sausage, chipotle grilled quail, and boar bacon. Dining on the patio is available in warm weather. $$

Banana Café
329 W. San Francisco St, Santa Fe, NM 87501
Tel: 505/982-3886
This Asian restaurant features Nouvelle Thai. Hints of lemongrass, basil, cilantro, coconut, peanuts, and chile are woven into traditional selections such as *pad Thai, tom yum gai,* and red and green curry. There's a nice mango chicken and spicy Balinese squid. $–$$

Café Pasqual
121 Don Gaspar St, Santa Fe, NM 87501
Tel: 505/983-9340 or 800/722-7672
This festive corner eatery has cuisine inspired by Mexican, Asian, and local Southwest traditions. Breakfast (served until 3pm) is the big draw, featuring signature dishes like *huevos motulenos* from the Yucatán peninsula, *huevos rancheros* with a rich red chile sauce, and the chorizo burrito. No reservations for breakfast. Get in line early. $$

Left: food fit for a cowboy (or girl)

Coyote Café
132 W. Water St, Santa Fe, NM 87501
Tel: 505/983-1615
Celebrity chef and cookbook author Mark Miller helped put Santa Fe on the culinary map and continues to delight diners with his Nouvelle Southwestern cuisine served up in a lively atmosphere. The star dish is the massive 'cowboy cut' chile-rubbed aged Angus beef ribeye, but the menu changes regularly. The rooftop Coyote Cantina (open in summer) and Cottonwoods, on the first floor, offer cheaper fare. **$$–$$$**

Chocolate Maven Bakery and Café
821 W. San Mateo, Santa Fe, NM 87501
Tel: 505/984-1980
Chocolate Maven's delectable brownies, scones, muffins, and other goodies can be found throughout Santa Fe. Place a special order early for the Belgian tortes and the signature carrot cake on holidays. Fluffy breakfast egg dishes and award-winning lunch-time soups are served in a pretty room adjoining the bakery. **$**

Geronimo
724 Canyon Rd, Santa Fe, NM 87501
Tel: 505/982-1500
Top-rated Geronimo occupies a warren of intimate dining rooms in a classic 1756 adobe building. While it can be pretty pricy, this 'Global-Fusion-Southwest' cuisine is definitely worth splashing out for. Elk tenderloin is a stand-out. A good tip is to eat lunch here for a fraction of the cost of dinner. Geronimo's owners also run Swig, a sophisticated nightclub and martini bar and the upscale Palace Restaurant. **$$–$$$**

Harry's Roadhouse
Old Las Vegas Highway, Santa Fe, NM
Tel: 505/989-4629
Sunday brunch at Harry's is a local tradition, but this lively roadhouse café is packed all day, and for good reason. The prices are low; portions of everything, from salads, burgers, and burritos to Moroccan couscous and curry, are generous; and wife Peyton's homemade pies, cakes, and crisps are to die for. Reservations recommended. **$–$$**

Pink Adobe
406 Old Santa Fe Trail, Santa Fe, NM 87501
Tel: 505/983-7712
Rosalea Murphy's restaurant – a Santa Fe tradition for 50 years – serves up well-prepared Continental and southwestern dishes. Try lamb curry, tamales, Gypsy Stew, and the charred New York strip called Steak Dunnigan. The packed Dragon Bar is *the* place to meet in town. **$–$$**

The Tea House
944 Palace, Santa Fe, NM 87501
Tel: 505/992-0972
This charming tea house in a rambling old family adobe offers 100 custom-blended teas, freshly baked scones, and light dishes. Scheduled entertainment, talks, and art exhibits. **$**

Top: in Santa Fe, dine under (and sometimes with) the stars

Abiquíu, Chama, and Ojo Caliente

Café Abiquíu
US 84, Abiquíu, NM 87510
Tel: 505/685-4378
Part of Dar Al Islam's attractive Abiquíu Inn, Café Abiquíu has Middle Eastern specialties as well as New Mexican *enchiladas, fajitas,* and *burritos.* Pies and cobblers are made with fresh fruit from the Chama River valley in season. Box lunches are available for hungry travelers with foodie tendencies. **$**

High Country Restaurant
Main St, Chama, NM 87520
Tel: 505/756-2384
This modest restaurant opposite Chama's historic train station has good down-home fare, ranging from juicy burgers and ribs to steaks and local trout. Good value. **$**

Rancho de San Juan
US 285, Ojo Caliente
Tel: 505/753-6818
A cozy fireside dining room is the setting for a beautifully presented, fixed-price, four-course meal at this elegant inn and restaurant in the serene foothills of the Ojo Caliente River valley. Recent selections have included grilled chipotle marinated tiger prawns with mango salsa and roasted rack of lamb with a Dijon-pepper crust. Desserts are works of art. A precious island of elegance in northern New Mexico's backcountry. **$$$**

Albuquerque

Conrad's
La Posada de Albuquerque
2nd St NW, Albuquerque, NM 87102
Tel: 505/242-9090
This hotel restaurant serves imaginative Southwestern fare and Italian dishes in an attractive Downtown dining room with starched linen tablecloths and attentive waiters. **$–$$**

Flying Star
Dietz Farm Plaza, 4026 Rio Grande Blvd NW, Albuquerque
Tel: 505/344-6714
With several locations in Albuquerque (including Nob Hill), Flying Star has something for everyone, from fabulous homemade soups, salads, and pizza to sandwiches, espresso, ice cream, and pastries. Browse a well-stocked magazine stand while dining and soak in the informal, artsy ambiance. **$**

Frontier Restaurant
2400 Central SE, Albuquerque, NM 87106
Tel: 505/289-3130
Don't leave the Duke City without enjoying a huge breakfast burrito smothered in hot chile at the city's best bargain eatery, opposite the University of New Mexico's main entrance. This 24-hour diner is an Edward Hopper classic, with 1950s Googie-style architecture and servers in white hats. The restaurant claims to serve 4,600 breakfast burritos per week and more than 7,000 tortillas a day. **$**

Range Café
4200 Wyoming Blvd NE, Albuquerque, NM 87111
Tel: 505/293-2633
The chefs at this good-natured restaurant treat such humble fare as chicken-fried steak, meatloaf, biscuits and gravy, chile stew, and *enchilada* with an attention to detail usually reserved for haute cuisine. The kitschy Western décor is a lot of fun. The original location is at 925 Camino del Pueblo in Bernalillo, north of Albuquerque heading towards Santa Fe; tel: 505/867-4755. **$–$$**

Top: dining can be outside and casual or inside and cozy

Scalo Northern Italian Grill
3500 Central Ave SE, Albuquerque, NM 87106
Tel: 505/255-8781
This longtime favorite on trendy Nob Hill features *osso bucco*, barbecued quail, salmon with dill sauce, tender squid, excellent pasta, and pizza. Pranzo in Santa Fe's Guadalupe District is under the same ownership. **$–$$**

High Road to Taos and the Rio Grande Valley

Embudo Station
P.O. Box 154 (off NM 68), Embudo, NM 87531
Tel: 505/852-4707
Housed in an old 19th-century railroad station among the cottonwoods on the banks of the Rio Grande, this restaurant is worth the drive. It serves a delectable selection of barbecued ribs, charbroiled steaks, grilled chicken, oak-smoked rainbow trout, and New Mexican dishes. Wash it down with green chile beer. Closed in winter. **$$**

Rancho de Chimayó
P.O. Box 11, CR 98, Chimayó, NM 87522
Tel: 505/351-4444
This family-run country restaurant in a lovely old *hacienda* is known for its good renditions of New Mexico classics. Quality has slipped in the face of run-away success but it still makes a nice place for an outing. **$–$$**

Trading Post Café
4179 Paseo del Pueblo Sur, Ranchos de Taos, NM 87557
Tel: 505/758-5089
Located just south of Taos, this restaurant features great food. The excellent pasta dishes include *penne arrabbiata*, snails with crispy angel hair, and *fettucine a la carbonara*. On the lighter side are a magnificent Caesar Salad and homemade chicken noodle or minestrone soup. **$–$$**

Taos

Bent Street Deli and Café
120 Bent St, Taos, NM 87571
Tel: 505/758-5787
Breakfast and lunch at this country-style café feature omelettes, fresh pastries, homemade soups, sandwiches, and salads made from organic produce. Dinner is a little more ambitious with seafood Provencal, lasagna, curried pork, and other dishes. The heated patio is a pleasant people-watching spot. **$–$$**

Doc Martin's
25 Paseo del Pueblo Norte, Taos, NM 87571
Tel: 505/758-2233
Housed inside the Historic Taos Inn, this is *the* place in downtown Taos for a night out. Dishes include maple-cured venison and entrees like seared salmon and roasted poblano pepper stuffed with duck confit and goat's cheese. The award-winning wine cellar showcases 400 wines. **$$**

Michael's Kitchen
305 Paseo del Pueblo Norte, Taos, NM 87571
Tel: 505/758-4178
A great place for all-day breakfast, Michael's is a popular local hangout. Lunch and dinner menus emphasize steaks, burgers, fried chicken, and New Mexican food. **$**

Momentitos de la Vida
P.O. Box 505, Arroyo Seco, NM 87514
Tel: 505/776-3333
The cuisine is described as 'New American' at this romantic country restaurant north of Taos on the Ski Valley road. The menu ranges from delicate smoked trout éclair and Louisiana blue crab cakes to plum-glazed duckling and saffron lobster risotto. Come with a good appetite. **$$**

Right: a spinach and chicken wrap

NIGHTLIFE

If you're looking for hot nightlife, then you'll be disappointed in Santa Fe. There's an incredible amount to do, but not much of it goes on past 10pm at night, when the streets get very, very quiet and folks retire behind thick adobe walls for personal party time. For big-city fun, Albuquerque is your best bet.

Things are improving in Santa Fe, though. Bars like Cowgirl, Evangelos, El Farol, La Fiesta Lounge in La Fonda Hotel, and El Paseo Bar open until the small hours. Café Oasis and the Atomic Grill are open until midnight. And dance clubs like Swig, Garrett's G Spot, The Paramount, and Rodeo Nites only start to heat up after 10pm.

July to September is the time when Santa Fe's world-famous Opera, Chamber Music, Symphony, and several theater seasons take place. Season-ticket holders quickly snap up tickets, so plan ahead if you're building your visit around the performing arts season. Santa Fe Opera tickets should be purchased well ahead of time by contacting the box office. Tickets for most sport and cultural events can be purchased by phone and in person at the individual box offices; from ETM Ticketing/Dillards (tel: 800/638-4253), Tickets.com (tel: 800/905-3315), and Ticketmaster (tel: 505/883-7800).

Entertainment listings can be found on Friday in *Pasatiempo*, the weekly arts supplement to the *Santa Fe New Mexican*, and *Venue*, the weekly supplement for the *Albuquerque Journal*. Also try the *Santa Fe Reporter* and the Albuquerque *Crosswinds* free papers, on Wednesday and Friday, respectively.

Major Venues
Santa Fe
Lensic Performing Arts Center
211 W. San Francisco St, Santa Fe, NM 87501
Tel: 505/988-1234
This beautifully restored 1931 movie palace is now a gorgeous performing arts center. It is the main performance venue in Santa Fe for eight major organizations. Youth concerts, classic movie showings, and community events happen in the daytime. Music promoter Jamie Lenfesty of Fanman Productions uses the Lensic for major touring acts (tel: 505/986-1858; www.fanmanproductions.com).

Paolo Soleri Outdoor Theater
Santa Fe Indian School, 1501 Cerrillos Rd, Santa Fe
Tel: 505/989-6300
Popular summer venue for big-name concerts under the stars.

Santa Fe Opera
Hwy. 285/84, Santa Fe, NM 87506
Tel: 505/986-5900 or 800/280-4654
Classics and new works are performed by renowned artists at this dramatic amphitheater north of Santa Fe. The season runs from late June/early July through August. Off-season performances are held at the Lensic and the St Francis Auditorium.

Top: licensed to serve alcohol

Albuquerque
Journal Pavilion
5601 University Blvd SE, Albuquerque
Tel: 505/452-5100
A huge new stadium venue for major concerts, just south of Albuquerque airport.

Sandia Casino Amphitheater
1–25 & Tramway Rd, Albuquerque, NM 87184
Tel: 800/526-9366
New Mexico's newest outdoor amphitheater at Sandia Pueblo attracts big-name acts.

KiMo Theater
423 Central Ave NW, Albuquerque, NM 87102
Tel: 505/768-3544
This landmark 1927 Pueblo Deco palace features a variety of live music acts.

Popejoy Hall
University of New Mexico, Center for the Arts, Albuquerque, NM 87131
Tel: 505/277-3824
New Mexico's largest multi-use theater is home to the New Mexico Symphony, Musical Theatre Southwest, and the popular Ovation series, which brings touring Broadway shows, ballet and modern dance companies, and other cultural programs to New Mexico.

Taos
Taos Center for the Arts
133 Paseo del Pueblo Norte, Taos, NM 87571
Tel: 505/758-2052

The premier venue in Taos, the center plays host to a wide variety of events, from classical music, Chinese acrobats, comedy troupes, and local theater to art exhibitions, all held at this facility near the Plaza.

Theater
Santa Fe Playhouse
142 E. De Vargas St, Santa Fe, NM 87501
Tel: 505/983-4262
Founded in 1922, the Playhouse is the oldest continuously running theater company west of the Mississippi. An annual Fiesta Melodrama satirizes the Santa Fe scene.

Santa Fe Stages
100 N. Guadalupe St, Santa Fe, NM 87502
Tel: 505/982-6683
June through September, this organization brings Broadway dance, music, theater, and other performances to the Lensic and the Armory for the Arts.

Classical Music
Santa Fe
Santa Fe Chamber Music Festival
P.O. Box 2227, Santa Fe, NM 87504
Tel: 505/983-2075
A summer concert series by resident and guest performers takes place at the Lensic and the St Francis Auditorium. Violinist Pinchas Zuckerman is one of the regulars.

Santa Fe Desert Chorale
P.O. Box 2813, Santa Fe, NM 87504
Tel: 505/988-7505
This chamber choir's repertoire ranges from medieval to avant-garde and many world premieres. Performances take place at the Santuario de Guadalupe, the Lensic, St Francis Cathedral, and other venues.

Santa Fe Pro Musica
P.O. Box 2091, Santa Fe, NM 87504
Tel: 505/988-4640 or 800/960-6680
This baroque and classical music series features well-known performers playing on early instruments. Concerts are presented at the Lensic, St Francis Auditorium, and other venues around Santa Fe. The season runs from September to April, but the baroque carol concerts in the beautiful Loretto Chapel are a Christmas highlight.

Left: Lensic Performing Arts Center

Santa Fe Symphony
P.O. Box 9692, Santa Fe, NM 87504
Tel: 505/983-3530
The symphony gives concerts at the Lensic from October to May.

Taos
Taos Chamber Music Festival
P.O. Box 1879, Taos, NM 87571
Tel: 505/776-2388
Associated with the acclaimed Taos School of Music, this series presents performances by world-class musicians at the Taos Community Auditorium.

Pop and Contemporary Music
Camel Rock Casino
Hwy. 285/84, Santa Fe, NM 87506
Tel: 505/984-8414
Golden oldie pop stars and comedians appear at this Tesuque Pueblo venue north of Santa Fe. Other Indian casinos offer big-name acts; contact individual tribes for information.

The Paramount
331 Sandoval St, Santa Fe, NM 87501
Tel: 505/982-8999
www.theparamountnightclub.com
Santa Fe's best small venue for national and international live music acts. The adjoining Bar B is used for intimate solo acts.

Dance
Aspen Santa Fe Ballet
550-B St Michael's Dr, Santa Fe, NM 87505
Tel: 505/983-5591
Santa Fe's hottest up-and-coming dance

troupe performs classical and contemporary repertoires at the Lensic.

María Benítez Teatro Flamenco
Radisson Santa Fe, 750 N. San Francisco Dr, Santa Fe, NM 87501
Tel: 505/955-8562
One of the world's best flamenco companies rivets audiences with its virtuosity. The company performs late June through August at a nightclub-style theater in the Radisson Hotel.

Film
Mainstream movies are shown at three Santa Fe multiplexes. Independents include:

CCA Cinematheque
Plan B Evolving Arts, 1050 Old Pecos Trail, Santa Fe, NM 87501
Tel: 505/982-1338
Santa Fe's best venue for small, artsy international movies. Has great popcorn.

The Screen
College of Santa Fe, 1600 St Michael's Drive, Santa Fe, NM 87505
Tel: 505/473-6494
Situated in the Moving Images Arts complex, the Screen is a state-of-the-art theater showing international and art movies.

Trans-Lux Jean Cocteau Cinema
418 Montezuma St, Santa Fe, NM 87501
Tel: 505/988-2711
A cozy little arthouse movie theater in the heart of the Guadalupe district.

Santa Fe Readings and Lectures
The winter/spring **Readings and Conversations** series at the Lensic is the premier place to see major international author lectures. The **James A. Little Theater** at the New Mexico School for the Deaf holds lectures by School of American Research archeologists and Los Alamos National Laboratory and Santa Fe Institute visiting scientists. **Recursos de Santa Fe** presents a writers conference, readings, and seminars at the Southwest Literary Center, tel: 505/982-9301, while **Southwest Seminars** offer public talks by experts on Southwest archeology and other topics at 6pm on Mondays at Hotel Santa Fe, tel: 505/466-2775.

CALENDAR OF EVENTS

Many events in Santa Fe and the surrounding area draw on a centuries-old Indian and Hispanic heritage. Each pueblo, for example, holds dances to celebrate the feast day of its patron saint and Christian holidays, which often coincide with solstice ceremonies observed as part of the seasonal agricultural calendar. Santa Fe Fiesta, celebrating the 1692 Reconquest of New Mexico by the Spanish, and the summer Indian and Spanish markets are the oldest community celebrations in the US. For more information, contact **New Mexico Department of Tourism** *(see page 99)*. For dates and times of dances, contact the **Eight Northern Pueblos** (tel: 800/793-4955).

January
Souper Bowl: Santa Fe restaurants compete for best soup and raise money for the Food Depot; tel: 505/471-1633

March
Rio Grande Arts & Crafts Festival: State Fairgrounds, Albuquerque; tel: 505/292-7457

April
Chimayó Pilgrimage: Christians walk to the Santuario de Chimayó, north of Santa Fe, on Holy Thursday and Good Friday to ask for Christ's blessings.

May
Cinco de Mayo: Festivals throughout the state celebrating Mexican liberation from French occupation.
Taste of Santa Fe: visitors pay to sample at this event; tel: 505/983-4823

July
Eight Northern Indian Pueblos Arts & Crafts: San Juan Pueblo; tel: 505/843-7270
Santa Fe Wine Festival: El Rancho de las Golondrinas, Santa Fe; tel: 505/471-2261
Spanish Market: Hispanic arts and crafts on Santa Fe Plaza; tel: 505/983-4038

August
Indian Market: SWIA puts on the country's largest competitive market of Indian art on Santa Fe Plaza; tel: 505/983-5220

Right: December *farolito* lights

September
Fiesta: The burning of Zozobra, religious observations, and community parades celebrate the Hispanic Reconquest of New Mexico, Santa Fe; tel: 505/988-7575

October
Albuquerque International Balloon Fiesta: The world's largest gathering of hot-air balloons staged over 9 days; tel: 800/733-9918

November
AID and Comfort Gala: Annual fundraising evening for people living with HIV/AIDS includes art auctions and entertainment at El Dorado Hotel, Santa Fe; tel: 505/989-3399

December
Santa Fe Film Festival: New Mexico celebrities come out for five days of premieres and screenings of new movies and award ceremonies at Lensic Performing Arts Center and other venues; tel. 505/988-5225
Todos Vamos a Belén: Traditional music and dance celebration starting Santa Fe's Christmas season; tel: 505/476-5100
Las Posadas: Traditional reenactment of Joseph and Mary's search for an inn, Santa Fe Plaza; tel: 505/476-5100
Canyon Road Farolito Walk: *Farolitos* (brown-bag) lanterns and *luminarias* (bonfires), plus strollers, musicians, and carolers, Santa Fe; tel: 505/984-6760

Practical
Information

GETTING THERE

By Air

A few commercial charters fly into **Santa Fe Municipal Airport** (tel: 505/955-2908), but most visitors arrive at the **Albuquerque International Sunport** (tel: 505/842-4366), just south of downtown Albuquerque. It's attractive and is served by most major airlines. There are 12 eateries, a sports bar, three gift and news shops, five cart vendors, a bank and ATM terminal, barber shop, shoeshine stand, meditation room, and exhibits of Indian art. Due to beefed-up post-9/11 security, you'll need to arrive two hours before your flight departs.

From the Airport

Santa Fe is 60 miles (96km) north of Albuquerque via Interstate 25, an hour's drive. The best solution to getting around New Mexico, a remote, rural state, is to rent a car at the airport. Major car-rental companies have desks inside the terminal, including economical Thrifty (tel: 800-367-2277) and Dollar (tel: 800-800-4000). Book in advance for best rates. If you're traveling in winter or driving offroad, consider a 4WD vehicle as many roads around Santa Fe are unpaved and get slick and muddy. To rent a car, you'll need to be at least 21 years old and have a valid driver's license and a major credit card.

Several shuttle vans do the run between Santa Fe and Albuquerque airport. **Sandia Shuttle** (tel: 888-775-5696) costs $23 each way and makes 10 trips a day, between 8:30am and 10:45pm from the airport, and between 5am and 10:45pm from Santa Fe. Call for reservations.

By Rail

Albuquerque and Santa Fe are on the main east–west route from Chicago to Los Angeles of **Amtrak** (tel: 800-872-7245). The Southwest Chief train arrives each afternoon at the Lamy train depot, 18 miles (28km)

southeast of Santa Fe. **Lamy Shuttle and Tours** (tel: 505/982-8829) will pick you up for $16 per person. Call for reservations.

By Road

Santa Fe is located at the intersection of Interstate 25, which continues north to Denver, Colorado, and US 285/84, which heads north through the Rio Grande Gorge to Taos and Colorado. You can pick up northbound I-25 from east-west-bound Interstate 40 at the 'Big I' junction in Albuquerque. NM 599 allows you to bypass Santa Fe and get on US 285/84, north of Downtown.

TRAVEL ESSENTIALS

Visas and Passports

You need a full, valid passport for entry to the US, and some visitors also need a visa. British and Canadian citizens, plus travelers from some European countries, do not need visas if they are staying less than 90 days and have a return ticket.

Customs

Everyone entering the country must go through US customs and security, a time-consuming process. To speed things up, pack items in see-through bags ready for inspection; leave weapons, pocket knives, and nail clippers at home; and be prepared to open everything, including laptop computers. You can import up to $10,000.

Left: Albuquerque stopover
Right: get your kicks here

Adults may bring in 1 liter (or quart) of alcohol; 200 cigarettes or 50 cigars (Cuban prohibited), or 4.4 pounds (2 kg) of tobacco; and gifts valued at under $400. Everything above this is taxed. Agricultural products, meat, and animals are subject to complex restrictions, especially if entering in California. For details, contact a US consulate or US Customs, www. customs.gov/travel/travel/htm.

Weather

Santa Fe has more than 300 days of sunshine a year. Average high temperatures reach the mid-80s°F (29°C) in summer. Nights are warm and pleasant, usually ranging from 60°F (16°C) to 70°F (21°C). Winter is chilly but often sunny, with highs averaging in the 40s°F (4–10°C), nighttime lows well below freezing, and occasional heavy snowfalls, particularly in January and February.

A prolonged drought has drastically reduced the amount of precipitation Santa Fe receives annually. In a good year, the City Different gets about 14 inches (36cm), almost all of it falling in daily heavy thunderstorms during the July–September summer 'monsoon' season, or as winter snow.

Clothes

Outdoor-casual or smart-casual clothing is your best bet. Wear breathable, lightweight garments layered on top of each other. If you head into the mountains, remember that temperatures drop sharply; carry a waterproof jacket, windbreaker, and/or warm wool or fleece sweater. Comfortable walking shoes are a must; hiking boots are best on mountain trails. In winter, bring a warm jacket, gloves, wool hat, and boots with good traction.

Dress-up outfits for women lean toward Indian- and Hispanic-influenced Santa Fe Style attire, such as ponchos and shawls, tiered velvet skirts and shirts, well-cut jeans, locally made cowboy boots, and Indian-made turquoise-and-silver jewelry. For men, jeans, cowboy boots, and *bola* string ties worn with Rio Grande-style woven waistcoats made in Chimayó are popular. Remember: less is more or you'll look like a tourist.

Electricity

The US standard is 110 volts, 60 cycle AC. Plugs have two flat prongs.

Time Differences

Santa Fe is on Mountain Standard Time, which is GMT –7 hours. It is 2 hours behind New York City and 1 hour ahead of Los Angeles. Daylight Savings Time (summer time) is observed.

GETTING ACQUAINTED

Geography

Santa Fe is located at 7,000ft (2,130m) in the western foothills of the 13,000-ft (4,000-m) Sangre de Cristo Mountains, the southernmost extension of the Rocky Mountains. The City Different sits on the eastern margin of the 30-million-year-old Rio Grande Rift Zone, a major volcanic fault running through central New Mexico. The rift is now occupied by the fabled Rio Grande, which has carved a deep gorge near Taos. West of Santa Fe are the Jémez Mountains, created by a massive volcanic explosion just over a million years ago. Volcanic activity also created the Cerrillos Hills and the Ortiz Mountains, located between the

Above: attire, especially on the ranches, is Southwest casual
Right: Santa Feans are a true cultural mix

Sangre de Cristo Mountains and Albuquerque's Sandia Mountains. This area is rich in turquoise, gold, silver, lead, and coal.

Population

In 2000, the combined population of the city and county of Santa Fe was 131,000 residents, with 63,000 living within the city limits. Hispanics are now a minority in the city – 47.8 percent; the rest of the population consists of non-Hispanic whites (46 percent) and other ethnic groups (3.2 percent). It speaks volumes about the attitudes and continuing influence of Hispanics on New Mexico culture that any non-Hispanic – from African-Americans to Jews and Tibetans – is considered an 'Anglo.' American Indians, the original New Mexicans, now comprise 3.1 percent of Santa Fe's population but are a highly visible presence, especially in contemporary arts.

How Not to Offend

Cultural sensitivity is vital in northern New Mexico, where, if you're Anglo, you'll probably be in the minority. Here are some things to bear in mind.

● New Mexico is officially bilingual – Spanish and English – so even a smattering of Spanish will instantly make people here more comfortable with you. Try to learn some phrases before leaving home.

● People of Hispanic heritage in New Mexico have various origins. Many can trace an unbroken, 400-year-old lineage to Spain and think of themselves as Spanish. Others are New Mexican *mestizo*, or mixed-blood,

Indian and Spanish. Still others may be more recent arrivals from provinces in Mexico, such as adjoining Chihuahua. Since you may not know a person's origin, it's best to use a catch-all term such as Hispanic (adjective or noun), Hispano (noun) or Latino (noun); Chicano is a contemporary term used in California and is not commonly used in northern New Mexico.

● Native American is a politically correct Anglo term. It's fine to use the term 'Indian' or better yet a person's tribal affiliation, e.g. Laguna, Taos, Jémez, or Picurís Pueblo, Jicarilla Apache, or Navajo.

● When visiting Indian pueblos and reservations, which are sovereign nations within the US, behave respectfully. Abide by all rules and regulations, including prohibitions on photography, sketching, taking notes, video and audio recording. A photography fee may be required. If you wish to take an individual's picture, you must ask permission first (a gratuity may be requested).

● Respect all restricted areas. These are usually posted. You'll usually need a permit to hike, hunt, fish, or drive around on back roads on Indian land. Never enter a home unless invited.

● Remember you are a guest on Indian land. Be polite and accommodating. Don't ask intrusive questions or interrupt during Indian ceremonies or dances. Even if an Indian event is not explicitly religious (such as a powwow), it may have a spiritual component. Show the same respect at Indian ceremonies that you would at any other religious service. At all events, try to maintain

a low profile, both in manner, conversation, and in dress (cover up and avoid shorts, bare arms, and flipflops).

• Keep in mind that Pueblo dances aren't performances scheduled for public viewing; they are religious ceremonies and you may attend only at the discretion of the tribe. Prepare for delays before events and call to check they are taking place.

• Finally, it is polite to accept if you are invited to eat in an Indian home. Extending hospitality to visitors and feeding them well is a long Indian tradition. Never offend your hosts by offering to pay for the food, and once you are finished eating, be sure to leave the table promptly. Many others will be fed that same day.

For more information, contact Albuquerque's excellent **Indian Pueblo Cultural Center** (1701 4th SW, Albuquerque; tel: 505/246-2261), which has exhibits on New Mexico's 19 pueblos, scheduled dances, demonstrations, and a restaurant serving Pueblo foods.

MONEY MATTERS

Currency

American currency uses the decimal system of dollars and cents (100¢ equals one dollar). There are $100, $50, $20, $10, $5, and $1 bills (notes), and $1, 25¢ (quarter), 10¢ (dime), 5¢ (nickel), and 1¢ (penny) coins. American bills and $1 and 25¢ coins are similar in size, so count your change.

Changing Money

Albuquerque airport has a bank where you can exchange foreign currency. Banks in Santa Fe will also do this for you. Be sure to bring your passport with you.

Traveler's Checks

American dollar traveler's checks can be exchanged without converting and incurring commission fees. Well-known brands of traveler's checks such as American Express can be used like cash in hotels, restaurants, and larger chain stores, but more and more, due to security concerns, you will be asked for photo identification such as a passport or a driver's license.

ATMs

ATMs (automatic teller machines) are located outside or in the lobby of most major bank buildings. In outlying towns you'll find them in shopping malls and supermarkets. If you're using a different ATM to your own bank, you'll be charged an additional $2–4 per transaction. An additional charge will then be levied by your own bank.

Credit Cards

Visa, MasterCard, Discover Card, and American Express are accepted in most but not all businesses. In Santa Fe and northern New Mexico, you'll encounter numerous street vendors and small businesses selling food, artwork, and other items who prefer cash. Most credit cards can be used to withdraw cash from an ATM (for a high fee) or to obtain cash advances over a bank counter.

Tipping

Tipping is customary and expected. Most New Mexicans in the service industry struggle to get by on low-paid work, so please be generous. Tip porters at airports and hotel bellhops $1 per bag. A doorman should be tipped if he unloads or parks your car (valet parking), usually about $1. Tip chambermaids if you stay several days in a hotel. Again, $1 a day would be appropriate. A tip of 15–20 percent of the bill before sales tax is the going rate for waiters, waitresses, bar staff, taxi drivers, and hairdressers.

Sales Tax

Santa Fe has a 6.6875 percent sales tax, which is added to the stated price of goods at the check-out counter. There are higher taxes for lodging and car rental in the city.

GETTING AROUND

Charter Vans and Tours

There are several good custom van tours around Santa Fe and to scenic outlying attractions, such as pueblo dances, parks, Taos, and O'Keeffe country. Among these are **Custom Tours by Clarice** (tel: 505/438-7116), **Art Colony Tours** (tel: 505/466-6146), and **Great Southwest Adventures** (tel: 505/455-2700). **Outback Tours** (tel:

800-800-JEEP) has Jeep eco-tours to the Jémez Mountains and beyond. **Southwest Safaris** (tel: 800-842-4246) offers unique one-day land-air tours to more distant attractions, such as Chaco Culture National Historical Park in northwestern New Mexico.

Public Transportation
Santa Fe Trails Transit System (tel: 505/955-2001) covers seven routes in downtown Santa Fe. Buses run Monday to Friday, 6am–10:30pm and Saturdays 8am–8pm, with limited service on Sunday and holidays. Most hotels have schedules, or you can pick them up at the Sheridan Street Transit Center, a block west of the Plaza.

Taxis
There's only one taxi company in Santa Fe, **Capital City Cab Company** (tel: 505/438-0000), but they'll take you anywhere.

Cars
Seat belts are required in New Mexico. You can make a right turn on a red light, provided there is nothing coming, there are no pedestrians in the crosswalk, or no sign prohibiting it. Speed limits are generally 25mph (40kph) in business districts, 30mph (48kph) in residential areas, and 55–75mph (88 or 160kph) on highways, as posted. Be careful driving in New Mexico. This state has one of the highest uninsured and drink-driving problems in the country, and accidents are common.

Parking
Downtown Santa Fe has a number of convenient municipal parking structures and plenty of two-hour parking meters on side streets. Feed meters regularly as wardens will issue a ticket for overdue meters (currently about a $5 fine), due within 10 days.

HOURS AND HOLIDAYS

Business Hours
Most banks open Mon–Fri 9am–5pm; some are also open Saturday mornings. Business hours are generally 8 or 9am to 5 or 6pm.

Shopping Hours
Santa Fe is a typical small southwestern desert city, where it seems like they roll the streets up and turn in after 9pm. Most stores are open from 9 or 10am to 6 or 7pm in Downtown locations, and until 9 or 10pm in the De Vargas and Villa Linda malls (shorter hours on weekends). In summer, businesses stay open later to accommodate tourists. Many Santa Fe galleries and museums open until 8pm on Fridays for receptions and entry to exhibitions.

Public Holidays
Most federal, state, and municipal offices, schools, and banks are closed on public holidays *(see page 94)*. Some holidays are celebrated on the closest Monday, in order to give people a long weekend. Some banks

Above: park your car and ride Santa Fe's excellent public transportation

and businesses close on Lincoln's birthday (Feb 12). In New Mexico, government and many business offices are closed on religious holidays, such as Good Friday and Christmas Eve, as well as for Santa Fe Fiesta, usually around Labor Day Weekend.

New Year's Day Jan 1
Martin Luther King Day third Mon in Jan
President's Day third Mon in Feb
Easter Sunday Mar or Apr
Cinco de Mayo May 5
Memorial Day last Mon in May
Independence Day July 4
Labor Day first Mon in Sept
Columbus Day second Mon in Oct
Veterans Day Nov 11
Thanksgiving Day fourth Thur in Nov
Christmas Day Dec 25

ACCOMMODATIONS

Accommodations in Santa Fe are pricy. The most popular lodgings often sell out a year ahead of time for Spanish and Indian markets, Fiesta, the Albuquerque International Balloon Fiesta, and Christmas. You'll get the best rate in the shoulder seasons (mid-Oct to Thanksgiving and Jan–Apr). Downtown Santa Fe has plenty of historic hotels, bed and breakfasts, and adobe *casitas* (small houses) within walking distance of the Plaza. There are lovely rustic spa resorts and bed and breakfasts near town, too. Many Santa Feans rent out private homes for the summer, beginning in July; check the *Santa Fe New*

Mexican (www.sfnewmexican.com) classifieds online before arriving. Most of the inexpensive chain motels are located down Cerrillos Road (NM 14), a busy and noisy thoroughfare several miles southwest of Downtown. If it's your first time in Santa Fe, stay Downtown. Locals may be able to get you a better rate.

For budget travelers, Santa Fe has the **Hostel International de Santa Fe**, located at 1412 Cerrillos Road (tel: 505/988-1153), which costs around $15 for a shared four-bunk-bed room (you are required to complete a work assignment). There is also good camping in Santa Fe National Forest below the Ski Basin in Hyde Memorial State Park. You'll need a car to get there.

$$$$ = over $200
$$$ = $150–200
$$ = $100–150
$ = under $100

Santa Fe Area
Adobe Abode
202 Chapelle Street, Santa Fe, NM 87501
Tel: 505/983-3133
www.adobeabode.com
Built in 1907 as an officers' quarters for Fort Marcy, this delightful adobe house is three blocks from the Plaza. The six attractive themed rooms and suites are comfortable. For extra privacy, ask for courtyard rooms behind the main house. Some rooms have fireplaces and patios. Full breakfast and afternoon sherry. **$$$**

Bishop's Lodge Resort and Spa
Bishop's Lodge Rd, Santa Fe, NM 87501
Tel: 505/983-6377 or 800-732-2240
www.bishopslodge.com
Bishop Jean Baptiste Lamy's 1851 personal retreat is now a luxury country resort on 1,000 acres (400 hectares) in the foothills of the Sangre de Cristo Mountains, 3 miles (5km) from the Plaza. Recently upgraded, it has more than 100 rooms and suites situated in 15 small lodges furnished in Pueblo or Spanish Colonial style. Tennis, swimming, fishing, hiking on nearby trails, and horseback riding. Full service spa. Gourmet restaurant. Shuttle to town. **$$$–$$$$**

Left: this historic estate is now a resort

Galisteo Inn

HC 75, Box 4, Galisteo, NM 87540
Tel: 505/466-8200
www.galisteoinn.com

It's worth the drive out of town to stay in this old *hacienda* in Galisteo Village, just east of the Turquoise Trail, in the Galisteo Basin. The chef encourages guests to pick their own veggies from the organic gardens (non-guests may also help out and receive a free lunch in the gourmet restaurant). It's a great place to relax and explore the basin's rich archeological history. $$–$$$

Garrett's Desert Inn

311 Old Santa Fe Trail, Santa Fe, NM 87501
Tel: 505/982-1851 or 800/888-2145
www.garrettsdesertinn.com

This motel, two blocks from the Plaza, has the most affordable rates around. You won't find chi-chi Santa Fe touches here, but the 76 standard rooms are comfortable, and six suites have small living rooms and kitchenettes with microwaves and small refrigerators. Limited wheelchair access. Onsite Avis Rent-A-Car and Camelot World Travel. Adjoining restaurant and dance club. $$

Hotel Santa Fe

1501 Paseo de Peralta, Santa Fe, NM 87501
Tel: 800-825-9876
www.hotelsantafe.com

Majority owned by Picurís Pueblo, this attractive, three-story Pueblo Revival-style hotel has 128 rooms and suites beautifully appointed in Southwestern style. All have microwave ovens, a stocked honor bar, phone modem, internet access, balcony or patio, and oversized king, double, and hideaway beds. The Hacienda, a luxury annex, has butler service. Public spaces feature original works of art; lectures by historians and archeologists on Monday evenings. Nightly Native American flute and guitar music by the *kiva* fireplace in the lobby. Gourmet restaurant, heated outdoor pool, and shuttle to the Plaza, five blocks away. $$–$$$$

Hyatt Regency Tamaya Resort and Spa

1300 Tuyuna Trail, Santa Ana Pueblo, NM 87004
Tel: 800/55-HYATT
www.hyatt.com

Spectacular Tamaya Resort is New Mexico's first high-end destination resort on Indian land. Chaco Canyon echoes strongly through the 350-room hotel's Great *kiva*-style layout and orientation to the cardinal directions. Rooms are large, plush, and all have balconies. Two championship golf courses, three swimming pools, a fitness center, and full-service spa, two superb restaurants, art-filled public spaces, and an onsite Santa Ana Pueblo museum. Cultural activities include Indian dancing, nature walks in restored woodlands along the Rio Grande, horseback riding on sacred lands, balloon rides, cooking classes, storytelling, and more. Shuttles transport guests to the tribe's casino. $$$–$$$$

Inn at Loretto

211 Old Santa Fe Trail, Santa Fe, NM 87501
Tel: 505/988-5531 or 800/727-5531
www.hotelloretto.com

Modeled after the terraced adobes of Taos Pueblo, the inn is a picturesque five-story structure two blocks from the Plaza. Guest rooms are furnished in regional style with hand-carved furniture, woven rugs, and Pueblo-style architectural details; some rooms have fireplaces and shared balconies. Full service spa. Gourmet restaurant. Tours. Access to Loretto Chapel. $$$–$$$$

Above: Hotel Santa Fe is majority owned by Picurís Pueblo

Inn of the Turquoise Bear
342 E. Buena Vista St, Santa Fe, NM 87501
Tel: 505/983-0798
www.turquoisebear.com
The former home of poet Witter Bynner is now a spacious adobe bed-and-breakfast villa with 10 guest rooms, many with tile or plank floors, fireplaces, and *viga* ceilings. Among the luminaries who have stayed here are Willa Cather, Ansel Adams, Igor Stravinsky, Edna St Vincent Millay, Robert Frost, W.H. Auden, Georgia O'Keeffe, and D.H. and Frieda Lawrence. For extra privacy, ask for the carriage house. **$$–$$$$**

La Fonda
100 E. San Francisco St, Santa Fe, NM 87501
Tel: 505/982-5511 or 800/523-5002
www.lafondasantafe.com
You'll get a glimpse of old Santa Fe at this famous 1920 Pueblo-style hotel on the southeastern corner of the Plaza. Each of the 167 rooms has its own individual – sometimes quirky – decor, with hand-painted furniture, tile murals, and other artsy touches. Some rooms have fireplaces and balconies. For an extra measure of luxury, ask for the rooftop suites on La Terraza. Traditional lobby, lounge bar, rooftop bar, gourmet restaurant, and tours. **$$$**

Pecos Trail Inn
2239 Old Pecos Trail, Santa Fe, NM 87501
Tel: 505/982-1943
www.travelhero.com
This pleasant motel on the quiet, residential, southeast side of town offers the city's best budget alternative to chain hotels on noisy Cerrillos Road. Of the 22 Southwest-style rooms, four are two-bedroom suites with living rooms and full kitchens; another four have kitchenettes. City park next door. Heated outdoor swimming pool; onsite restaurant. Harry's Roadhouse restaurant and Museum Hill are five minutes away. **$**

Out of Town
Abiquíu
Abiquíu Inn
P.O. Box 120, Abiquíu, NM 87510
Tel: 505/685-4378 or 800/447-5621
www.abiquiuinn.com

This pleasant inn near the Chama River is part of the Dar Al Islam property and is the area's best deal. Guests can choose *casitas*, rooms, or suites with kitchens. Large *casitas* accommodate four and have full kitchen, woodstove or fireplace, hand-tiled bath, and separate bedrooms. Onsite café. O'Keeffe Home tours leave from adjoining office. **$$**

Ghost Ranch Education & Retreat Center
HC 77, Box 11, Abiquíu, NM 87510
Tel: 505/685-4333 or 877/804-4678
www.ghostranch.org
Owned by the Presbyterian Church, Ghost Ranch offers no-frills lodging ranging from dormitory-style rooms to bare-bones *casitas*. Two museums, cafeteria, hiking trails, residential workshops, and retreats. A second campus is located in Santa Fe, on the corner of Paseo de Peralta and the Old Taos Highway. **$–$$**

Albuquerque
La Posada de Albuquerque
125 Second St NW (at Copper Ave), Albuquerque, NM 87102
Tel: 505/242-9090 or 800/777-5732
www.laposada-abq.com
Built in 1939 by New Mexico native Conrad Hilton, the nine-story La Posada remains one of downtown Albuquerque's most popular boutique hotels. An attractive two-story Pueblo Revival-style lobby features traditional dark-varnished wood, hand-painted murals, fountains, and a lively bar. Guest rooms have TVs, telephones, data ports, and A/C. Elegant gourmet restaurant, and it's all within walking distance of Downtown. **$$–$$$**

Los Poblanos Inn
4803 Rio Grande Blvd NW, Albuquerque, NM 87107
Tel: 866/344-9297
www.lospoblanos.com
Housed in a beautiful 1930s John Gaw Meem hacienda, Los Poblanos sits on 25 acres (10 hectares) of lavender fields in the idyllic North Valley. Six rooms are arranged around a peaceful courtyard. There is a separate guest house suitable for families and a large adjoining cultural center with Peter Hurd murals. Innkeepers Penny and Armin

Rembe are easy-going, well-informed hosts, and their huge collection of Southwest art fills every corner. Authentic Mexican breakfasts are served in a bright, cheerful room. **$$–$$$$**

High Road to Taos
Rancho Manzana
Tel: 888/505-2277
www.ranchomanzana.com
This lovely bed and breakfast inn occupies a 250-room adobe *hacienda* on the south side of Chimayó's historic Plaza Cerro. Rooms have four-poster beds, comforters, and antiques. There are also organic gardens, cooking classes, and an annual lavender festival in May. **$$**

Ojo Caliente
Ojo Caliente Spa and Resort
50 Los Baños Dr, Ojo Caliente, NM 87549
Tel: 800/222-9162
www.ojocalientespa.com
Located at one of the oldest health resorts in North America, this 1916 Mission Revival hotel has a porch with rockers and rustic rooms with toilets and sinks, but no phones or TVs. Guests bathe in the bathhouse of the adjoining hot springs. Newer cottages have more privacy and amenities. Full service spa; free hot springs access. Onsite restaurant offers light spa fare as well as New Mexico cuisine. **$$–$$$**

Rancho de San Juan
US 285, Ojo Caliente, NM 87549
Tel: 505/753-6818
www.ranchodesanjuan.com
Refined Southwestern style is evident in every corner of this *hacienda*-style compound, surrounded by 200 acres (80 hectares) in the Rio Caliente Valley. Seventeen guest units include standard rooms and *casitas* with fireplaces, all with phones and baths. Many designer touches and antiques. One of the top restaurants in New Mexico (open to non-guests). **$$$–$$$$**

Santa Fe Trail
Plaza Hotel
230 Plaza, Las Vegas, NM 87701
Tel: 505/425-3591 or 800/328-1882
www.plazahotel.com

The 36 rooms in this restored Victorian hotel have a faded frontier elegance. The restaurant and bar are a popular local rendezvous, particularly for Sunday brunch, which features live Spanish guitar music. Complimentary continental breakfast. Business center. In-room massage. **$$**

St James Hotel
17th and Collinson sts, Cimarron, NM 87714
Tel: 800/748-2694
Built in 1872 by Henri Lambert, personal chef to Abraham Lincoln and General Ulysses S. Grant, this classic Western hotel is one of the most infamous in New Mexico. Among the notables who stayed here were gunmen Jesse James, Clay Allison, and Blackjack Ketchum (who is buried in nearby Clayton). Several ghosts haunt the hotel, with Lambert's wife the most frequent visitor. Rooms are modest but authentic. No phones or TVs. The motel annex has more amenities but little charm. Restaurant, coffee shop, and bar. **$$**

Taos
El Monte Sagrado
317 Kit Carson Rd, Taos, NM 87571
Tel: 800/828-8267
www.elmontesagrado.com
Opened in July 2003, owner Tom Worrell's exotic eco-resort three blocks from downtown Taos has 37 elegant suites overlooking

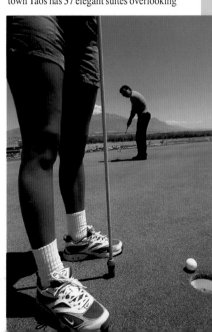

Right: Twin Warriors Golf Course at Hyatt Regency Tamaya Resort

a healing circle in the center of the property. The sumptuous, oversize rooms are decorated in American Indian and international themes. Sustainable design, employed whenever possible, includes buildings made from recycled materials and an elaborate water purification system. Local organic produce and free-range bison and yak in the restaurant from Worrell's own ranch. Full-service spa and healing workshops. Twelve *casitas* in renovated historic adobes sleeping 2–8 are located nearby. $$$$

Historic Taos Inn
125 Paseo del Pueblo Norte, Taos,
NM 87571
Tel: 505/758-2233 or 888/518-8627
www.taosinn.com
Opened in 1936, the Pueblo Revival-style inn is built around 19th-century family adobes on a historic *placita*. Attractive Southwestern rooms have fun and individual touches; many even have *kiva* fireplaces. There's a bar with live music and a gourmet restaurant with excellent wine. $$–$$$

Mabel Dodge Luhan House
204 Morada Lane, Taos, NM 87571
Tel: 505/751-9686
www.mabeldodgeluhan.com
This lovely bed and breakfast inn is the former home of Mabel Dodge Luhan, socialite and patron of the arts. Small but attractive rooms once occupied by D.H. Lawrence, Georgia O'Keeffe, and other notable guests have low *viga* ceilings, adobe walls, carved furniture, and bathrooms. The two most popular rooms are those atop the main house, which were used by Mabel Dodge and her Taos Pueblo husband Tony; these have bathroom windows painted by D.H. Lawrence and Dorothy Brett. It's a popular venue for meditation, writing, and arts workshops. Memorable breakfasts at shared tables in the Italian-style dining room feature organic produce. $$–$$$

HEALTH AND EMERGENCIES

It is essential to have health insurance in the US, as all medical and dental services are extremely expensive. High-altitude living also takes a little getting used to. Even fit visitors may experience shortness of breath in Santa Fe. Don't overdo exercise until your body adjusts. Good sun protection is important, as Santa Fe and the surrounding high-desert mountains receive far less protection from the sun's rays than at sea level. Use sunscreen with an SPF rating of 15 or higher, and wear a broad-brimmed hat and polarized sunglasses.

Keep a water bottle with you, and drink plenty of water throughout the day. Cut back on caffeine and alcohol, which are both dehydrating. Don't drink untreated water from streams while hiking. It often contains giardia, a nasty bug that can cause bloating, stomach upset, diarrhea and other disorders.

24-Hour Emergency Numbers
Dial 911 for police, fire, and ambulance.

COMMUNICATIONS

Mail Services

There are post offices in De Vargas and Villa Linda malls in Santa Fe. The main post office is at S. Federal Place, a block north of the Plaza. It's open 7:30am–5:30pm, weekdays, and 8am–1pm Saturday. If you need to mail packages back home, look for the nearest branch of Mail Boxes, Etc., which will pack and ship your goods for a small extra charge. It also offers Federal Express and UPS service.

Telephone

The area code for Santa Fe and the rest of New Mexico is **505.** It's not necessary to dial the area code for local calls within the city and county of Santa Fe and to Los Alamos. All other calls are long distance. For either local or long distance information, dial **411.** For a toll-free number dial 1-800-555-1212. Many hotels add a high service charge to long-distance calls made from your room, so try the lobby.

Newspapers

Santa Fe's daily newspaper is the *Santa Fe New Mexican*. The *Albuquerque Journal* includes a daily *Journal North* section covering northern New Mexico. Both newspapers have good entertainment listings and articles every Friday. Santa Fe's free alternative paper, the *Reporter*, appears on Wednesday. Albuquerque's free alternative paper, *Crosswinds*, is available in Santa Fe on Fridays. *New Mexico* magazine appears monthly, as does the *Santa Fean*, an upscale lifestyle magazine.

Radio

KSFR (90.7FM), broadcasting out of Santa Fe Community College, carries National Public Radio (NPR), BBC news, and a broad range of interesting local programming, from *Goddess Radio* to high-kicking Spanish-language *salsa* shows.

Radio shows on KUNM (89.9FM) broadcast from the University of New Mexico, include the nationally syndicated *Native America Calling* morning show, as well as NPR and community programming. Santa Fe's KBAC (98.1FM), otherwise known as

Radio Free Santa Fe, has popular DJ personalities who play a great combo of classic and adult contemporary music and live studio appearances by visiting musicians.

Television

All four national networks – ABC, NBC, CBS, and FOX – are carried in Santa Fe via their Albuquerque station affiliates. The local Public Broadcasting Service (PBS) station is KNME. A large choice of cable and satellite channels is available.

TOURIST INFORMATION

Santa Fe Convention and Visitors Bureau is located in the Sweeney Convention Center (201 W. Marcy St; tel: 505/955-6200 or 800/777-2489; www.santafe.org; open Mon–Fri 8am–5pm). The **New Mexico Department of Tourism**, Santa Fe Welcome Center, is located in the Lamy Building (491 Old Santa Fe Trail; tel: 505/827-7400 or 800/545-2040; www.newmexico.org; open daily 8am–5pm, until 7pm in summer).

Tours

Companies offering walking tours of Santa Fe include **Aboot About/Santa Fe** (tel: 505/988-2774); **Historic Walks of Santa Fe** (in La Fonda Hotel, tel: 505/986-0122); and **Loretto Tours** (in Inn at Loretto, tel: 505/983-3701). In summer, docents from the Museum of Fine Arts and the Palace of the Governors offer tours.

USEFUL INFORMATION

Travelers with Disabilities

For information on places in Santa Fe conforming to the Americans with Disabilities Act (ADA) specifications, pick up a copy of *Access Santa Fe* from the New Mexico Tourism office in the Lamy Building.

Travelers with Children

Santa Fe is an historic town with an older population, and not especially child friendly. Kid-oriented attractions like children's museums and Albuquerque's Explora! are detailed in each specific itinerary.

Left: chiles to go

ACKNOWLEDGEMENTS

Photography	
22	**Christian Heeb**
71	**George H.H. Huey**
2/3	**Liz Hymans/Corbis**
25, 75	**IndexStock/Photolibrary.com/**
13B	**Catherine Karnow**
87	**Bob Krist**
10, 14B, 15	**Library of Congress**
	Museum of New Mexico
13T, 14T	J.R. Riddle, neg no 38211
62B	John Candelario, neg no 165660
1, 5, 8/9, 11, 12, 16T&B, 20, 21, 23T&B,	**Richard Nowitz**
24T&B, 26T&B, 27, 28, 29, 31, 32,	
33T&B, 34T&B, 35, 36T&B, 37, 38T&B,	
39, 41T&B, 42T&B, 43, 44, 45T&B, 46,	
47, 50, 51, 52T&B, 53, 54, 55, 546, 57,	
58, 59T&B, 60, 61, 62T, 63, 64, 65T&B,	
66T, 67, 68T&B, 69, 70T&B, 72, 73T&B,	
(74) 76, 77, 78T&B, 79, 80, 81, 82, 83, 84,	
84, 86, 88, 90, 91, 93, 94,	
95, 97, 98, 100	
66B	**Stephen Trimble**
Front cover	**Table Mesa Prod/Index Stock/**
	Photolibrary.com
Cartography	**Mapping Ideas Ltd**

INDEX

Abiquíu 14, 63–5
accommodations 94–8
airports 89
Albuquerque 15, 21, 74–5
    BioPark 75
    Explora! Science Center 75
    KiMo Theater 75
    Maxwell Anthropology Museum 75
    Museum of Art and History 74
    New Mexico Museum of Natural History
        and Science 75
    Nob Hill 75
    Old Town 74
    Angel Fire ski resort 60
Apaches, the 14, 64, 71
Arroyo Seco 59
art and artists 11, 13–7, 24, 25, 28, 29, 31–4,
    36, 37, 39, 41, 42, 43, 46, 47, 51, 53–8, 60–4,
    68, 72–5
Aztecs, the 72

Bandelier, Adolph 15, 33, 35, 44
Bandelier National Monument 42, 43, 44
birds and bird-watching 21, 34, 39, 69, 71
Bishop's Lodge Resort & Spa 40
Black Mesa 42, 47
Blue Lake (Taos Mountain) 59

Camino Real Trail 26
camping 53, 94
Capulin Volcano National Monument 71
Carson, Kit 14, 55–6, 71
Carson National Forest 67
Carson Nation 53
Cerillos 11, 72
    Cerillos Hills Historic Park 72
    Clear Light Opera House 72
    Cerillos Historic Mining District 72
Chaco, the 43
Chama 65–7
Chimayó 51, 53
    Chimayó Museum 51
    Santuario de Nuestro Señor de Esquipulas
        51
Chiripada Winery 54
Cochiti Pueblo 44, 47
Cochitis, the 47
Colorado Plateau 65
Comanches, the 14, 17, 51, 63
Cordova 53
Cumbres and Toltec Scenic Railroad 66

Dance and dancing 37, 43, 46, 47, 60, 86
Dar Al Islam 64
D.H. Lawrence Ranch 60–1

Eagle Nest Lake 60
eating out 80–3
Echo Amphitheater 65
E.E. Fogelson Visitor Center 68
**Eight Northern Indian Pueblos Visitors
    Center** 63
Elizabethtown 60
emergencies 98
Enchanted Circle 60
Española 43, 62

Festivals 87
Forked Lightning Ranch House 68
Fort Marcy 14, 39–40
Fort Union 14, 69–70
Frijoles Canyon 44

Galisteo Basin 72
Gallinas Canyon 69
Ganados del Valle cooperative 66
Garden of the Gods 72
Georgia O'Keeffe Home 64
GeorgiaO'Keeffe Museum 25
Ghost Ranch 4, 17, 25, 26, 31, 38, 40, 65
    Florence Hawley Ellis Anthropology
        Museum 65
    Ruth Hall Paleontology Museum 65
Glorieta Pass and Mesa 67–8
golf 42, 46
Golden 73

Hewett, Edgar Lee 15, 17, 28, 42
History 11–17
Hollywood Casino 47
horseback riding 40, 46
hotels 94–8
Hyatt Regency Tamaya Resort and Spa 46
Hyde Memorial State Park 34

Independence 14
Indian Pueblo Cultural Center 92

Jémez Mountains 42, 43, 44, 45, 46, 47, 53
Jémez Pueblo 45, 46, 68
    Walatowa Visitor Center 46
Jémez Springs and Bath House 45
Jémez State Monument 45

Kasha Katuwe Tent Rocks National Monument 47
Kid, Billy the 23
Kiowa National Grasslands 70
Kit Carson Home and Museum 71
Kozlowski's Stage Stop 68
Kruger, W.C. 36

La Cienega 47
La Fonda Hotel 26, 27
Lamy, Bishop Jean-Baptiste 25–6, 31, 38
Lamy Building 35
Las Trampas 53
  San Jose de Gracia Church 53
Las Vegas 69
  Haye Springs Well 69
  Las Vegas National Wildlife Refuge 69
  Plaza Hotel 69
  Rough Riders Museum 69
Lawrence, D.H. 33, 55, 56, 60–1
Lensic Performing Arts Center 27, 84, 85
Lew Wallace Building 35
Lobo Mountain 60
Loretto Chapel 26
Los Alamos 15, 17, 43
  Bradbury Science Museum 43

Madrid 72–3
Maxwell National Wildlife Refuge 71
media 99
Meem, John Gaw 27, 28, 29, 31, 32, 57, 64, 68, 75
Mesa Verde 45
Mills Canyon 70
Missionaries 13
Monastery of Christ in the Desert 64
Montezuma Castle 69
music 85–6

National Park Service –Southwest 29
Nature Conservancy 34
Navajos, the 14, 29, 32, 64
nightlife 84–6
New Mexico State Capitol, Santa Fe 35

Ogapoge 12
Ojo Caliente Hot Springs and Spa 67
O'Keeffe, Georgia 24, 25, 54, 55, 61, 62, 64, 65, 75, 79
Ok'he 63
  O'Ke Oweegne Arts and Crafts Cooperative 63
Old Pecos Trail 28, 67

Old Santa Fe Trail 28, 67
de Oñate, Juan 12, 17, 62–3
Orilla Verde National Recreation Area 54

Palace of the Governors 11, 13, 14–15, 17, 23–24
Pecos 68
Pecos National Historical Park 68
Pecos Wilderness 40
Pedernal 65
Penasco 53
de Peralta, Pedro 12, 17
performing arts 84–5
Picurís Pueblo 53
Picurís Pueblo Museum 53
San Lorenzo de Picurís Church 53
Pilar 54
Pojoaque Pueblo 41
Poeh Cultural Center 42
population 91
Poshouingue 63
Prince, Bradford 14, 15, 23
public holidays 93–4
public transportation 93
Pueblo Revolt 17, 25, 35, 46, 51, 63
Puye Cliff Dwellings 43

Railyards, Santa Fe 16, 37, 77
Randall Davey Audubon Center 34
Rancho de los Golondrinas 47
Ranchos de Taos 53
Redondo Peak 45
Red River 60
restaurants 80–3
Rio Grande Gorge 54, 67
Rio Grande Gorge Bridge 58
Rio Grande Visitor Center 54
Rough Riders Museum, Las Vegas 69
Route 66 15, 46, 75

Sandia Crest Scenic Byway 73
Sandia Mountains 53, 91
San Diego Canyon 45
San Felipe Pueblo 47
San Francisco de Asís Church 53
Sangre de Cristo Mountains 16, 21, 40, 67
San Ildefonso Pueblo 42
San Juan Mountains 65, 67
San Juan Pueblo 62, 63
Santa Ana Pueblo 46
Santa Ana Star Casino 46
Santa Clara Pueblo 43
Santa Cruz 62

Santa Fe
art galleries 79
Bataan Memorial Building 36
Barrio Analco 35
Children's Museum 28
Christmas Eve Farolito Walk 32
Cristo Rey Church 31
Cross of the Martyrs 25
Farmer's Market 16, 37
Georgia O'Keeffe Museum 25
Governor's Gallery 36
Governor's Mansion 40
Guadalupe–Railyards 37–8
Immaculate Heart of Mary Seminary 32
Institute of American Indian Arts 25
El Museo Cultural 37
Loretto Chapel 26
Lensic Performing Arts Center 27
Museum of Fine Arts 17, 24
Museum of Indian Arts and Culture 28
Museum of International Folk Art 28
Museum of New Mexico 17, 23, 79
Museum of Spanish Colonial Arts 28, 79
oldest house 35
Plaza 22
New Mexico State Capitol 35
St Francis Cathedral 12, 17, 25
St John's College 29, 34
Visitors and Convention Bureau 35, 99
Wheelwright Museum of the American
    Indian 29
Santa Fe Canyon Preserve 34
Santa Fe National Forest 41
Santa Fe Opera 40
Santa Fe Southern Railway 37
Santa Fe Trail Museum 70
Santo Domingo Pueblo 47
Santuario de Nuestro Señor de Esquipulas
    51
Santuario de Nuestra Señora de Guadalupe
    38
Scottish Rite Temple 39
shopping 77–9
skiing 39, 53, 58, 60, 73
Spanish-American War 69

Tamaya 46
Taos, the 53, 56
Taos 15, 21, 55–60
Bent Home and Museum 56
E.L. Blumenschein Home and Museum 56
Fechin Institute 57
Harwood Museum of Art 57
Kit Carson Home and Museum 55
Mabel Dodge Luhan House 55
Millicent Rogers Museum 58
Van Vechten-Lineberry Collection 58
Taos Society of Artists 56, 57, 58, 75
Taos Canyon and Ski Valley 56, 58, 60
Taos Mountain Film Festival 59
Taos Pueblo 59, 60
Church of San Gerónimo 60
Mountain Casino 59
taxis 93
Tecolote Mountains 68
telephones 99
Ten Thousand Waves spa 39
Tesuque 40, 41, 51
theater 85
Tierra Amarilla 65, 66
Tinkertown 73
Tlaxcalan, the 35
tourist information 99
tours 92–3
Towa, the 62, 68
trains 89
Treaty of Guadalupe-Hidalgo 14
Tres Piedras 67
Truchas 53
Turquoise Trail 11, 72
Tusas Mountains 67
Tyuonyi Pueblo 44

United World College 69
University of New Mexico 75
Utes, the 14, 64, 71
Ute Indian Wars 64

Valles Caldera National Preserve 43–5
de Vargas, Diego 13, 17, 25, 62
Vasquez de Coronado, Francisco 12, 17
Velarde 54
Vermejo Park Ranch 70
Vietnam Veterans National Memorial 61
visas and passports 89

Walatowa Pueblo 45, 46
walking and hiking 34
weather 90
Wheeler Peak 60
white-water rafting 21
wildlife 39, 42, 70, 75
World War I and II 15

Zaguán, El 32
Zia Pueblo 46